BIG-NOTE PIANO

Best of JOHN WILLIAMS

ISBN 978-1-4803-4325-2

HAL•LEONARD®
CORPORATION
7777 W. BLUEMOUND RD. P.O. BOX 13819 MILWAUKEE, WI 53213

Visit Hal Leonard Online at
www.halleonard.com

CANTINA BAND

from STAR WARS: EPISODE IV - A NEW HOPE

Music by
JOHN WILLIAMS

Fast Ragtime

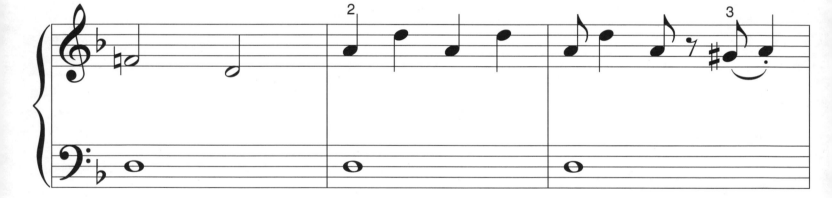

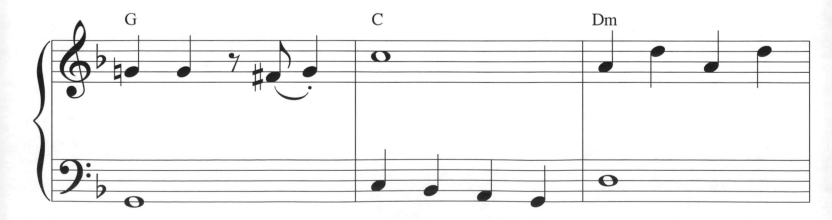

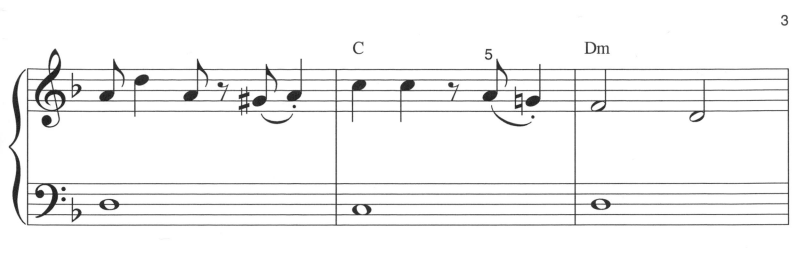

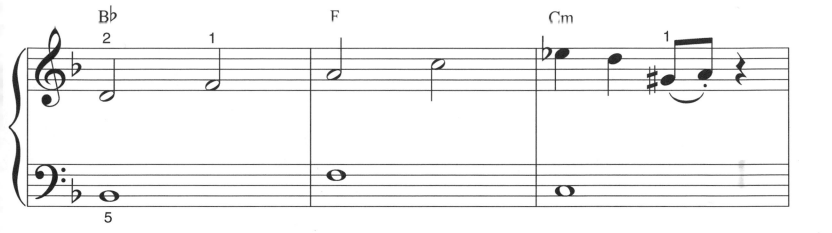

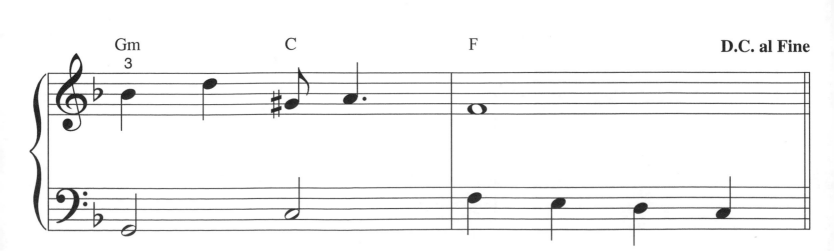

ACROSS THE STARS
Love Theme from STAR WARS®: EPISODE II - ATTACK OF THE CLONES

Music by JOHN WILLIAMS

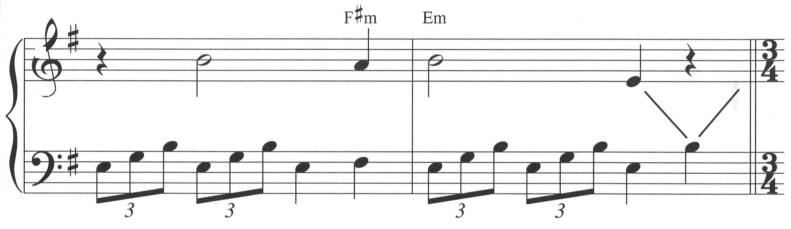

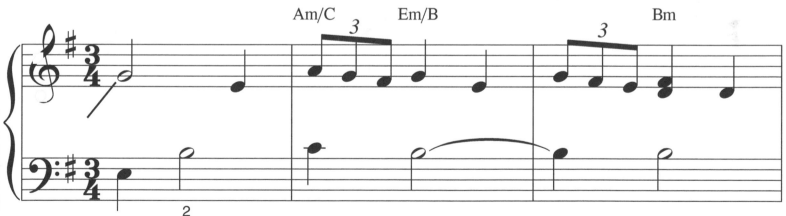

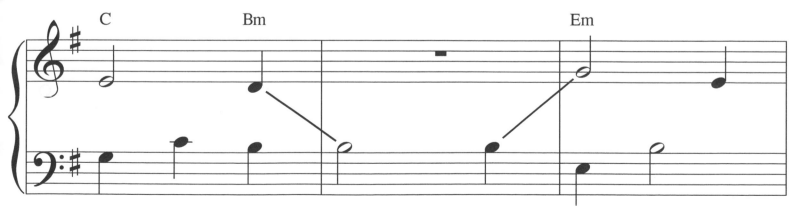

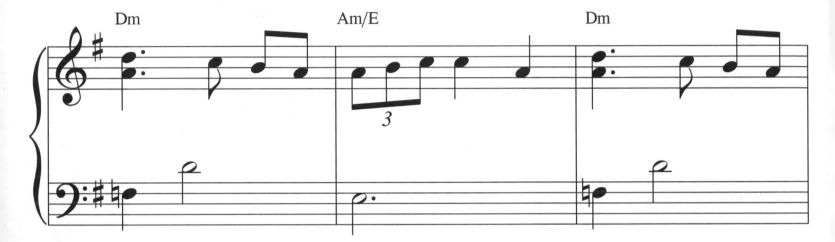

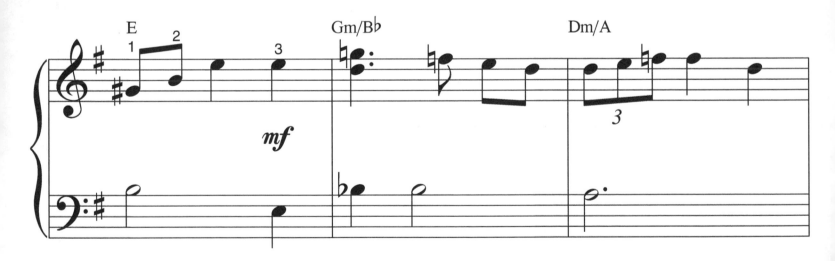

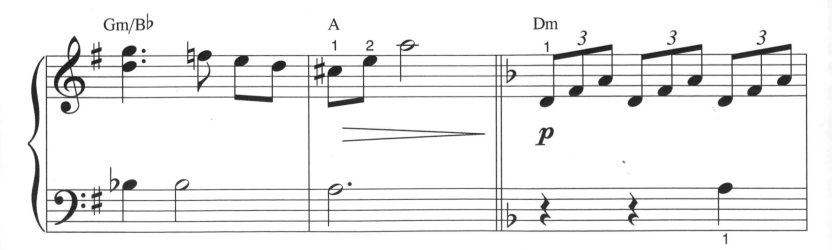

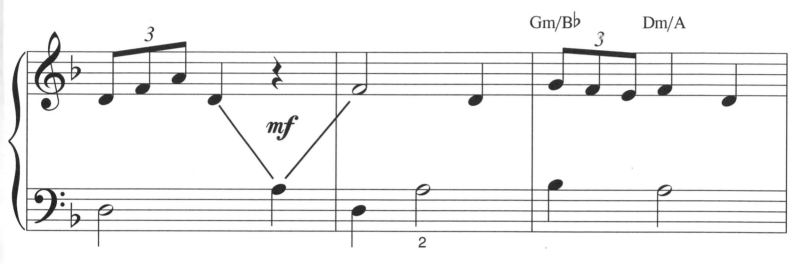

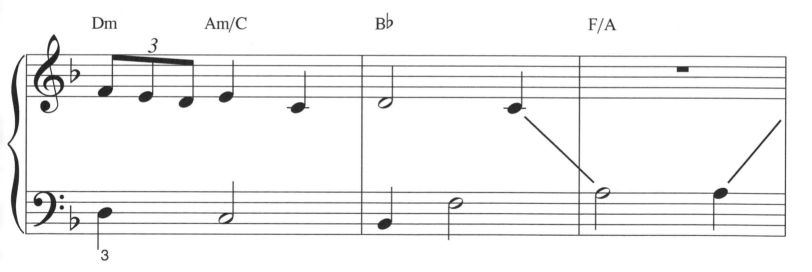

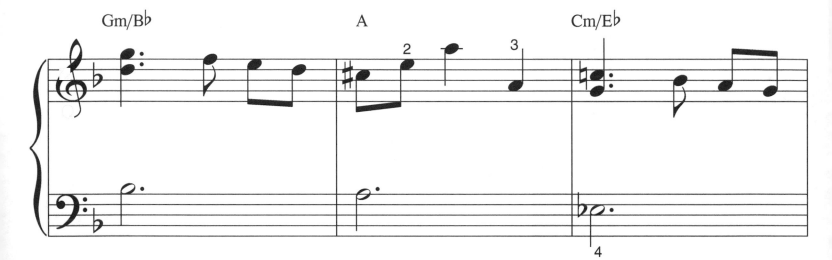

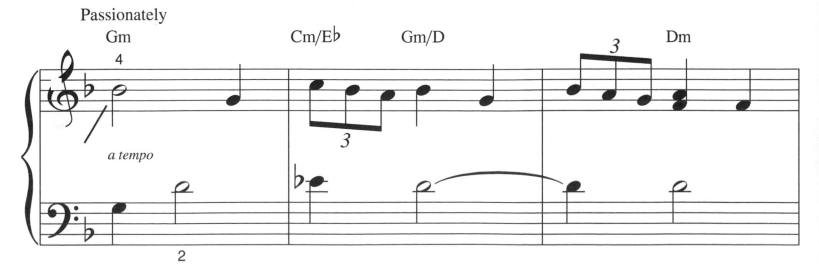

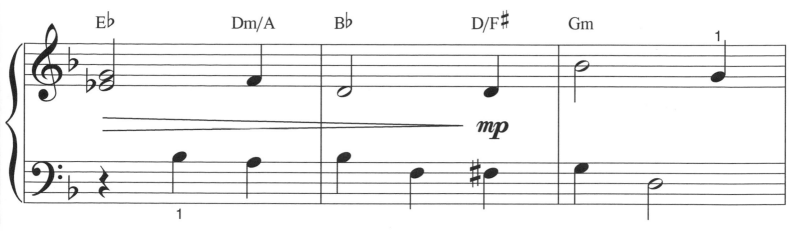

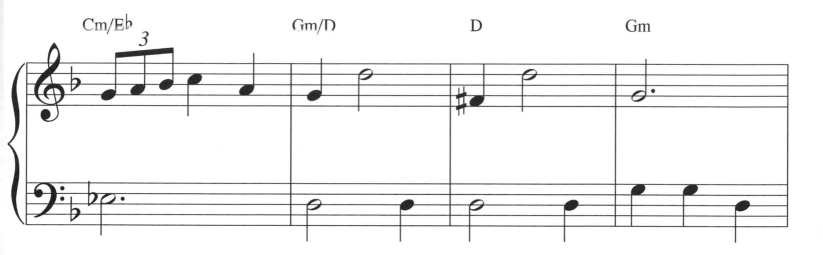

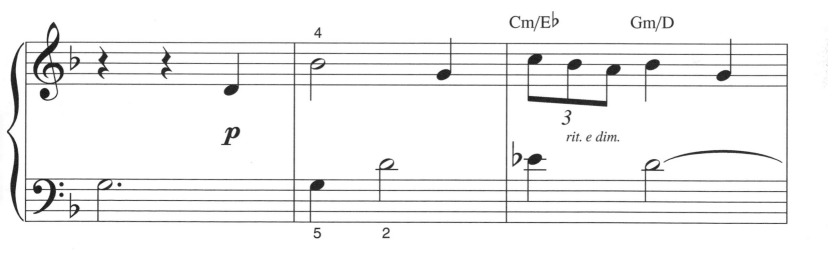

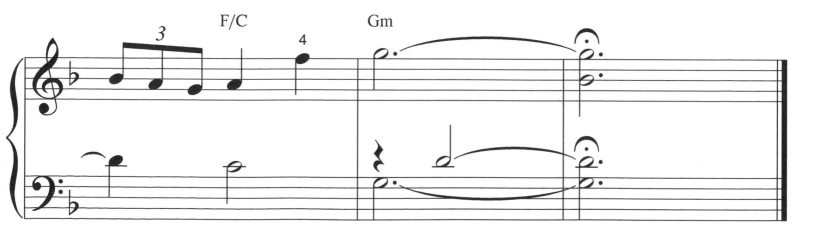

Can You Read My Mind?
Love Theme from SUPERMAN

Music by JOHN WILLIAMS
Words by LESLIE BRICUSSE

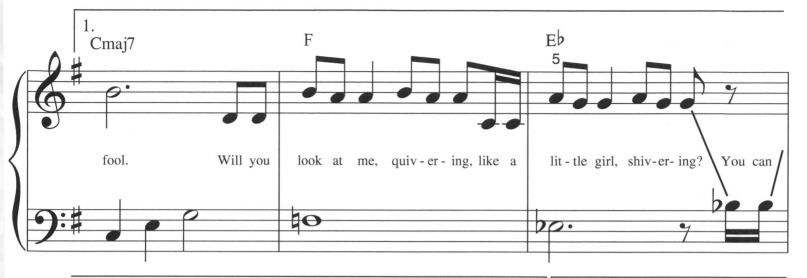

fool.   Will you   look at me, quiv-er-ing, like a   lit-tle girl, shiv-er-ing?   You can

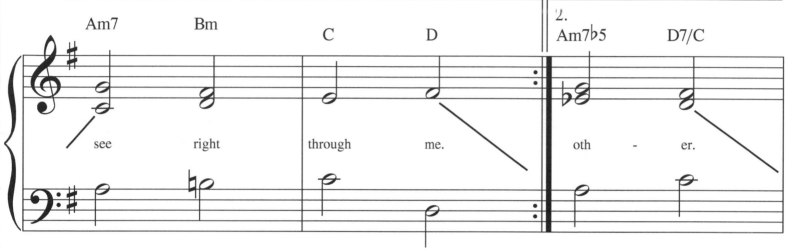

see   right   through   me.   oth - er.

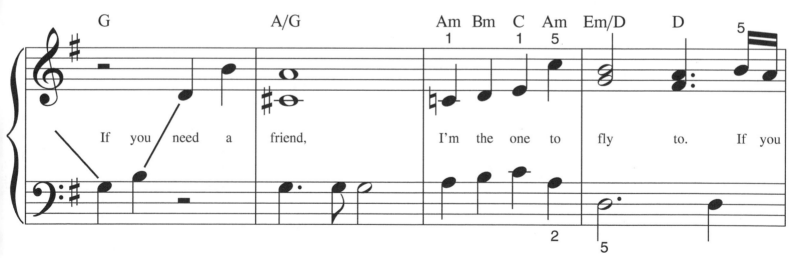

If   you   need   a   friend,   I'm the one to   fly   to.   If you

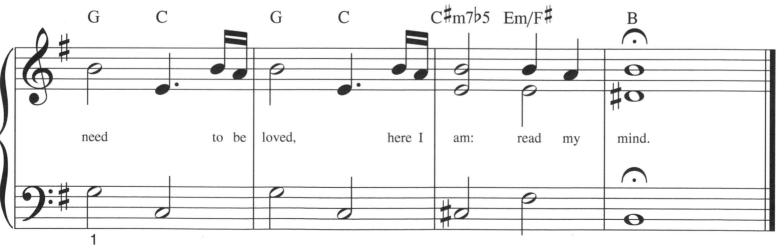

need   to be   loved,   here I   am: read my   mind.

THEME FROM
CLOSE ENCOUNTERS
OF THE THIRD KIND

By JOHN WILLIAMS

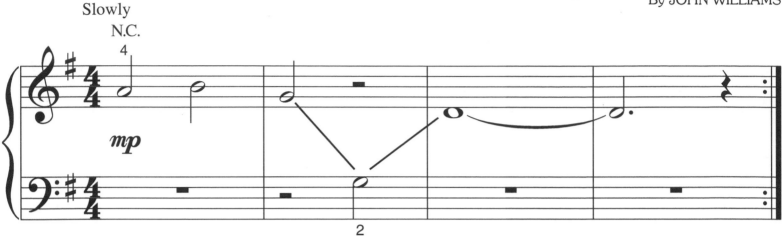

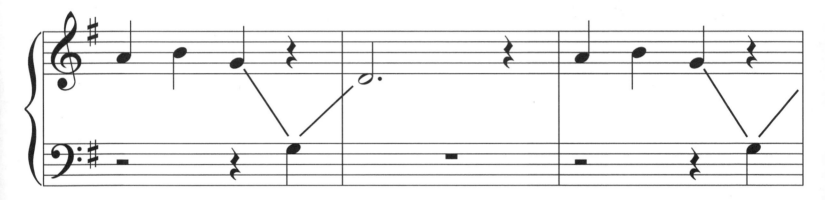

With more motion

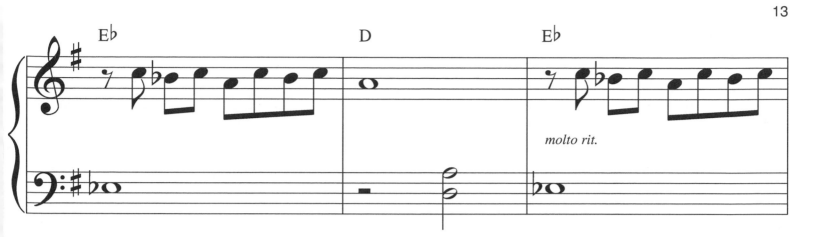

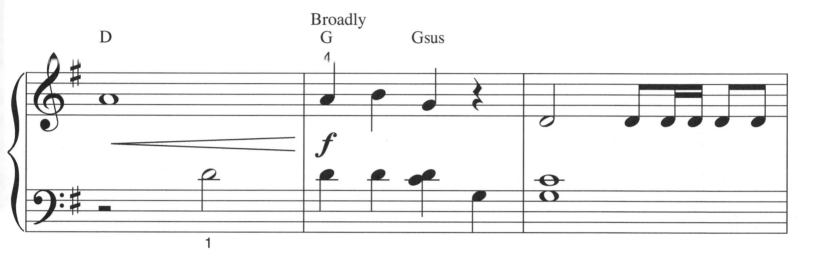

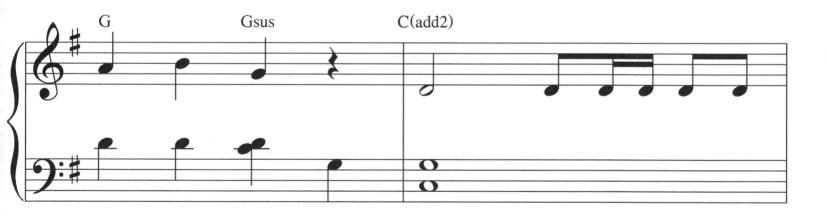

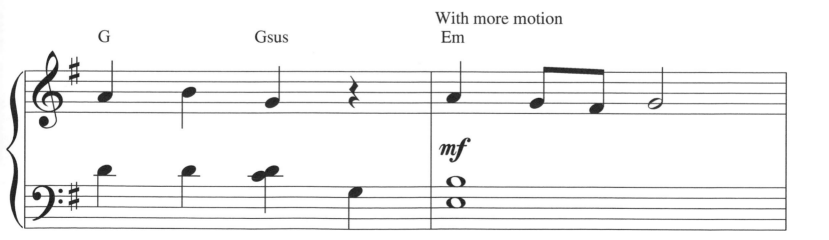

14

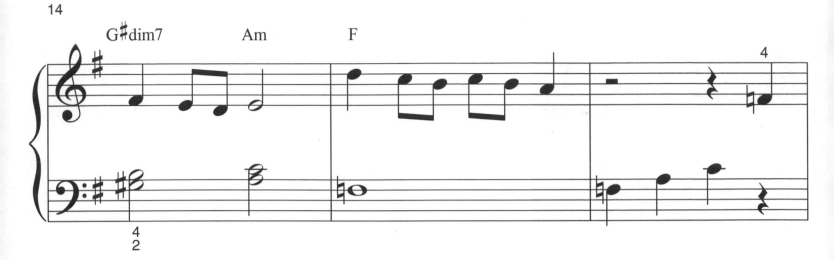

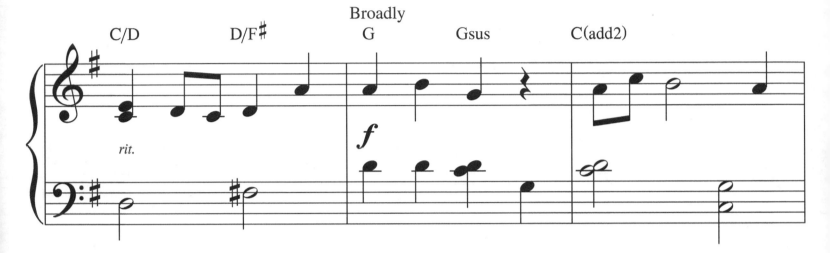

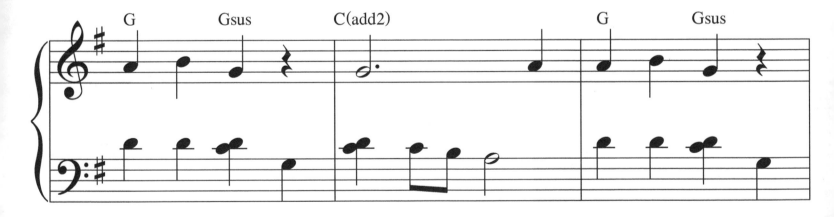

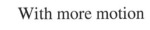

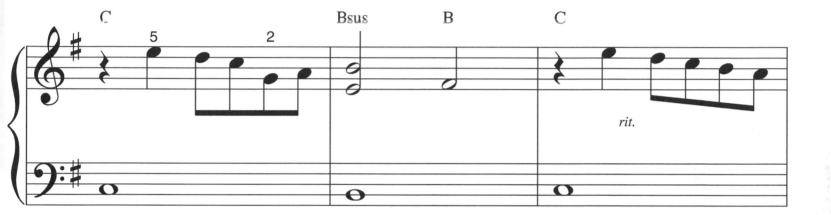

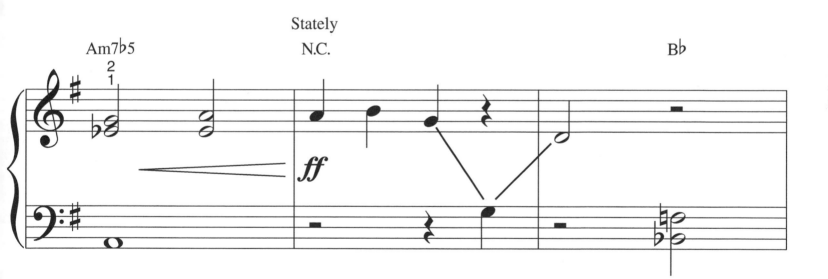

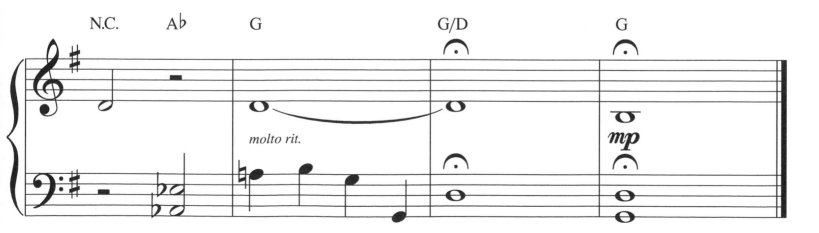

THEME FROM E.T.
(The Extra-Terrestrial)
from the Universal Picture E.T. (THE EXTRA-TERRESTRIAL)

Music by
JOHN WILLIAMS

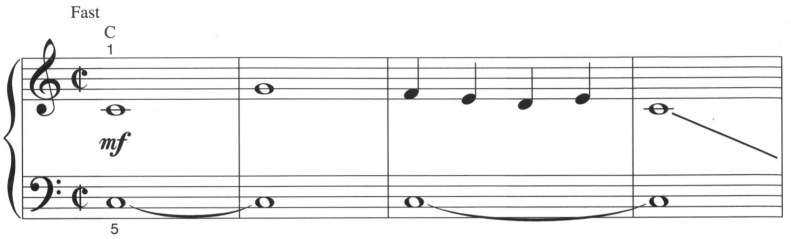

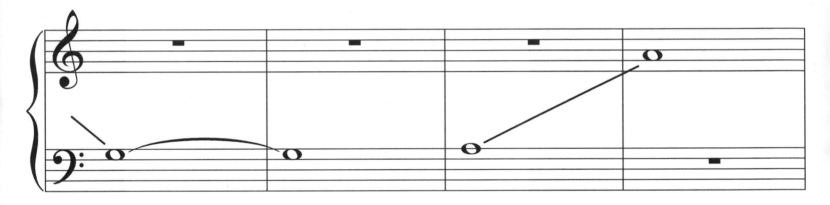

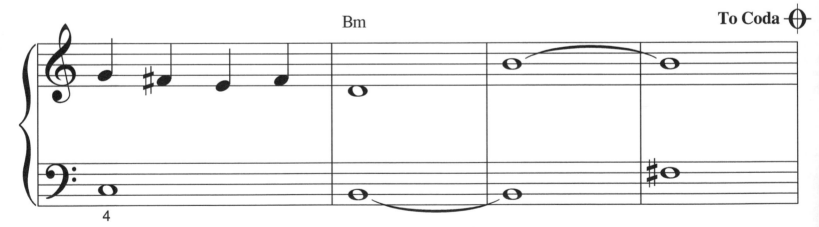

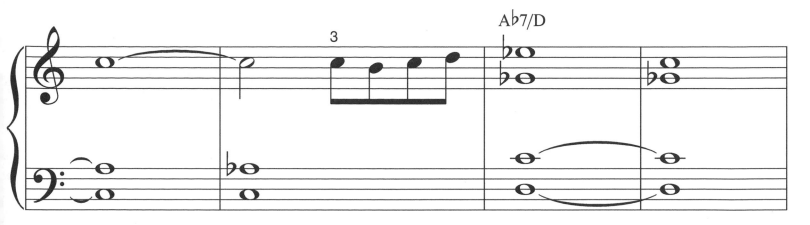

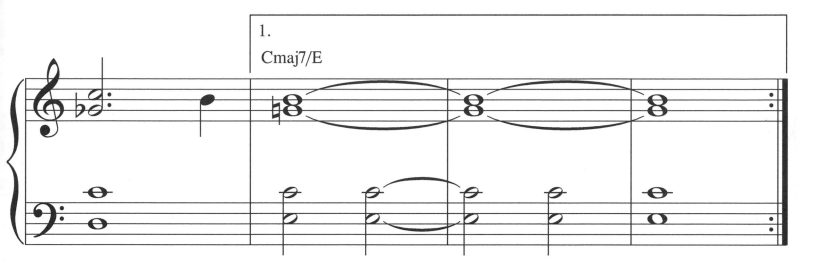

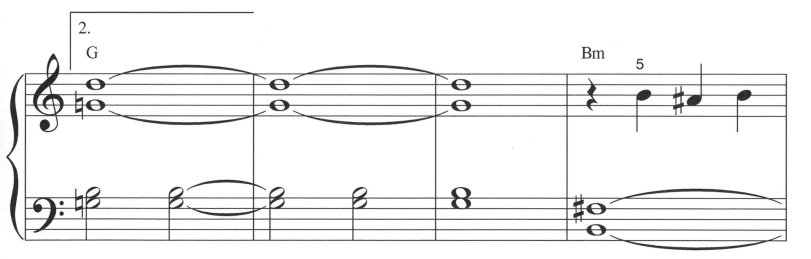

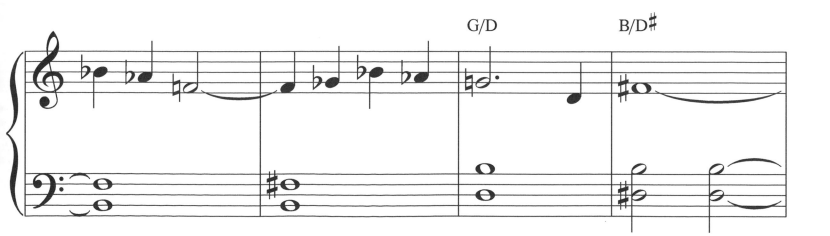

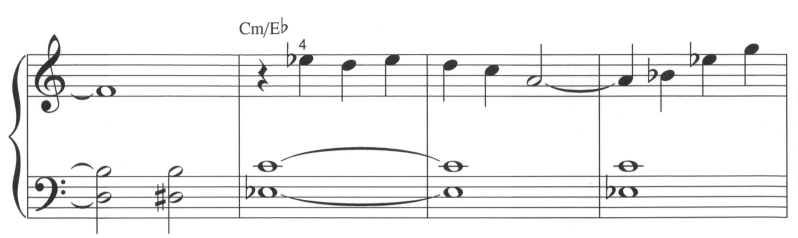

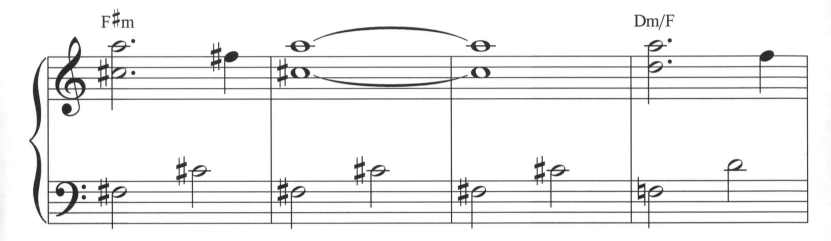

CODA

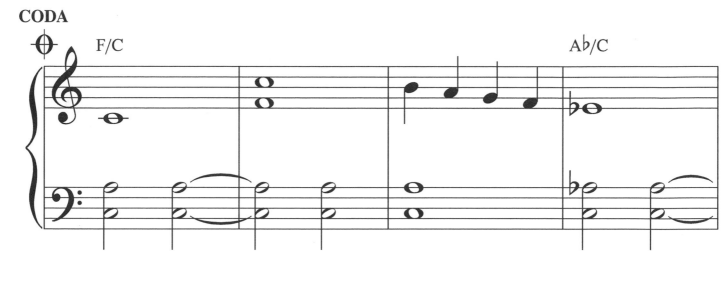

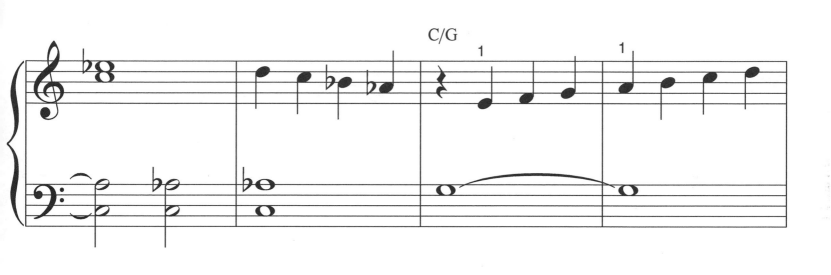

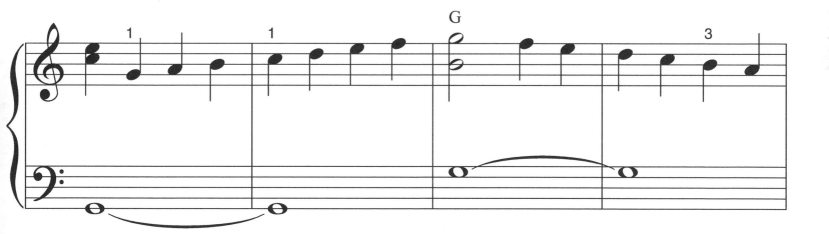

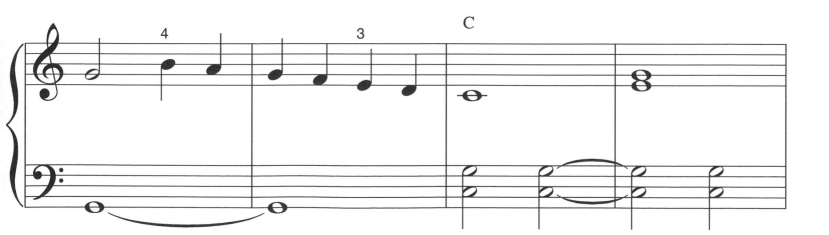

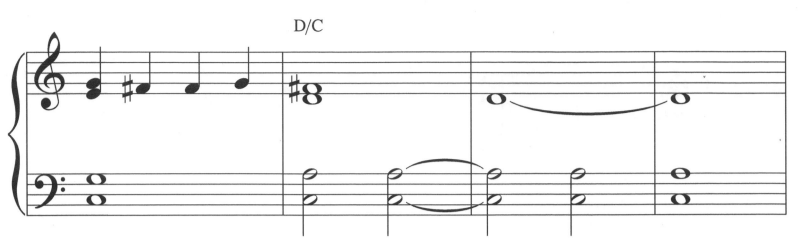

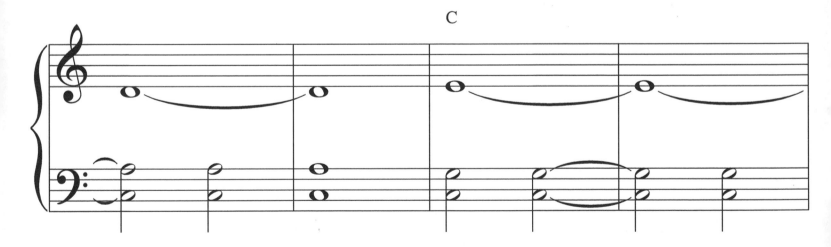

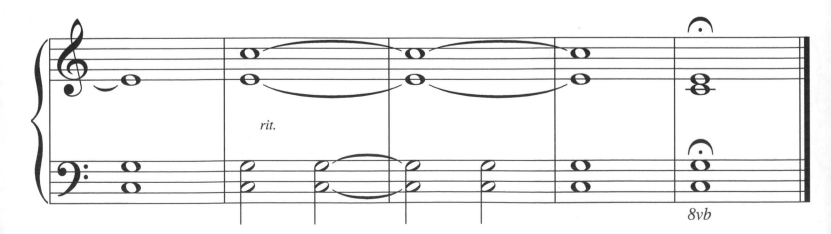

HEDWIG'S THEME
from the Motion Picture HARRY POTTER AND THE SORCERER'S STONE

Music by
JOHN WILLIAMS

Mysteriously

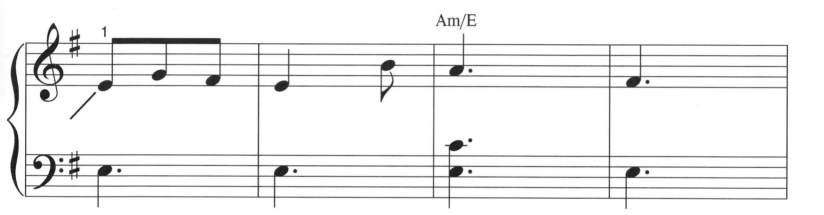

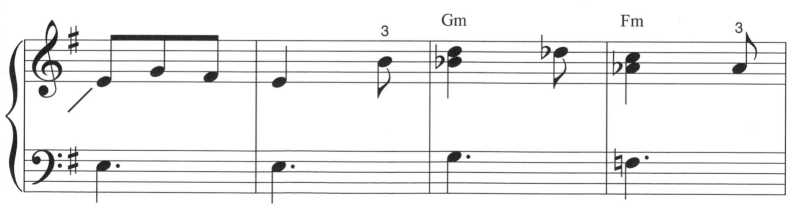

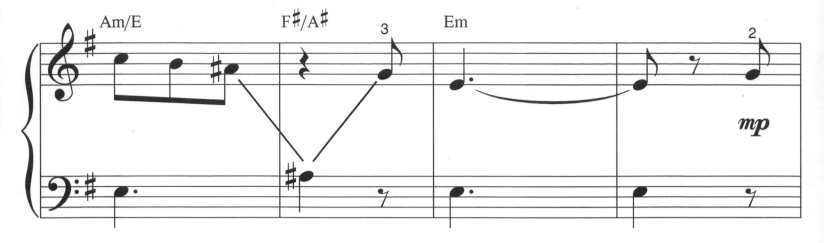

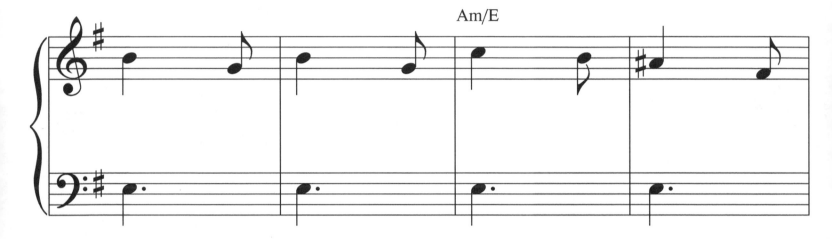

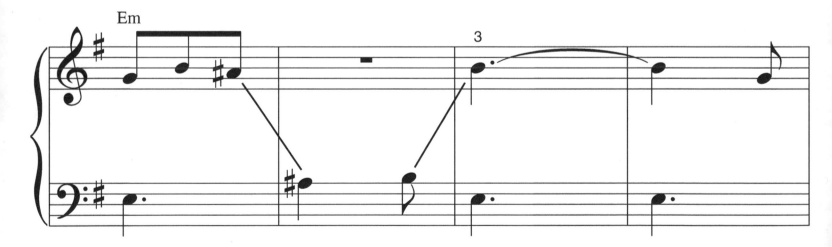

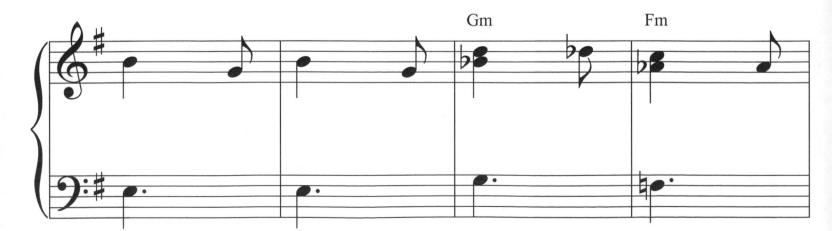

23

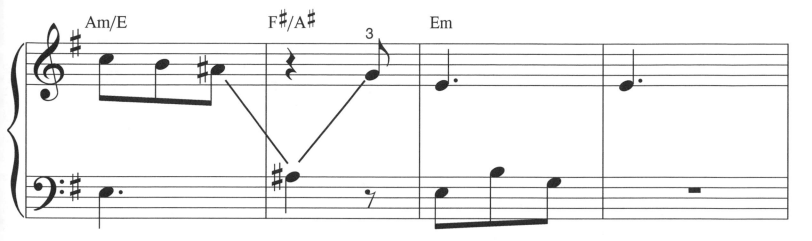

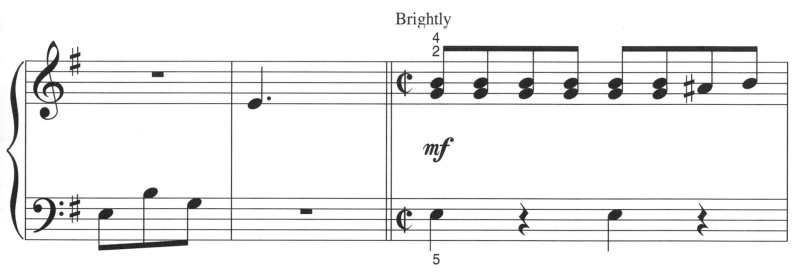

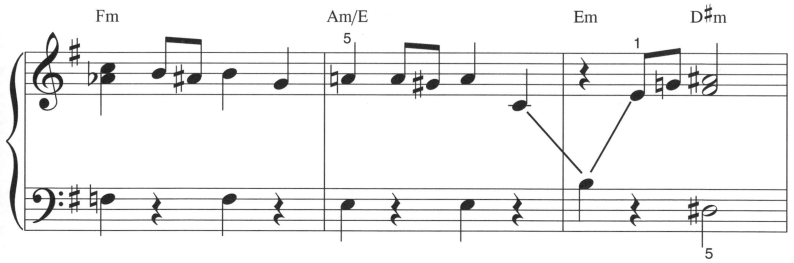

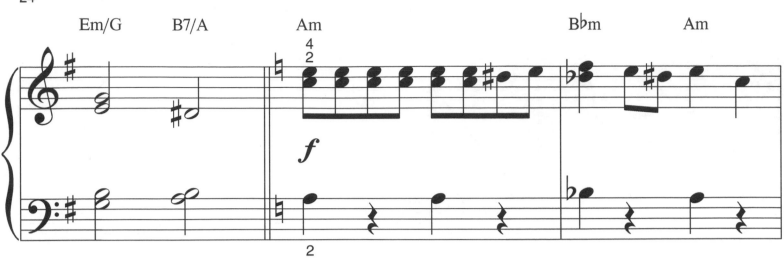

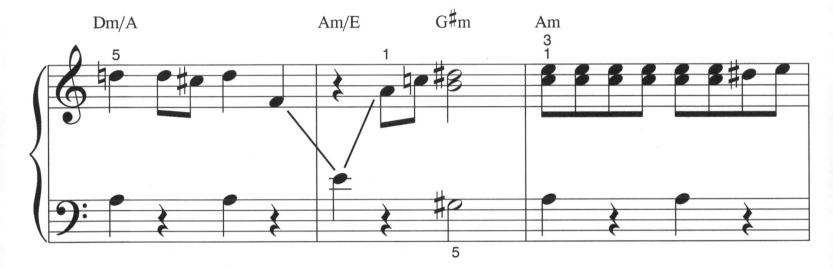

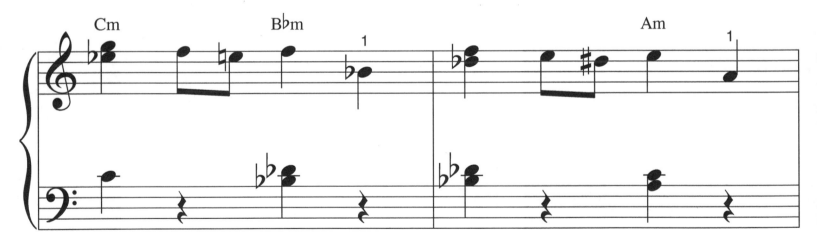

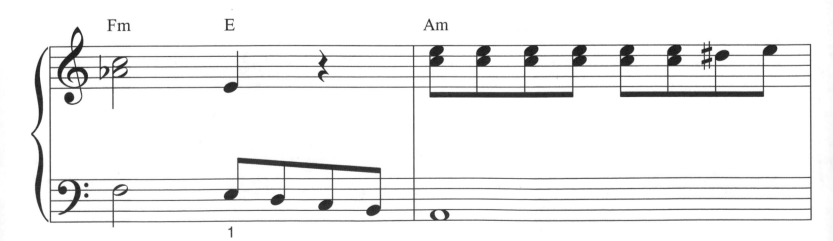

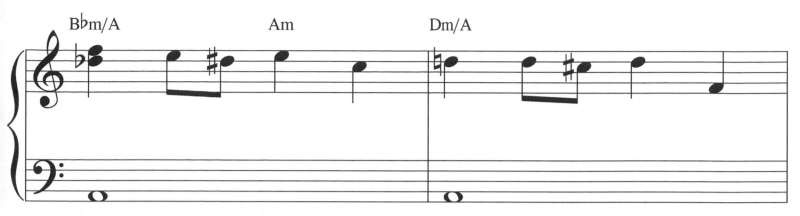

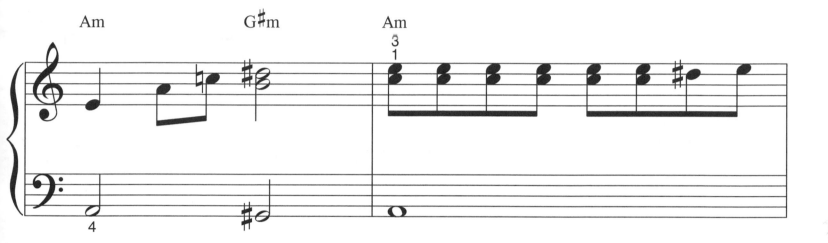

HARRY'S WONDROUS WORLD

from HARRY POTTER AND THE SORCERER'S STONE

By JOHN WILLIAMS

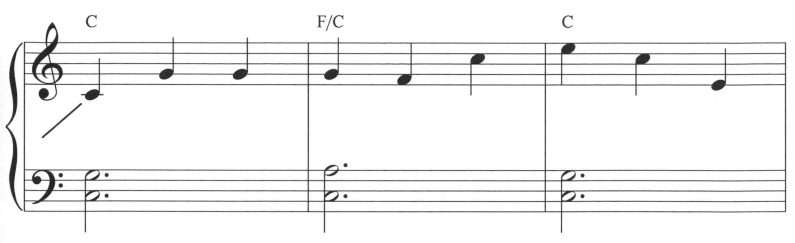

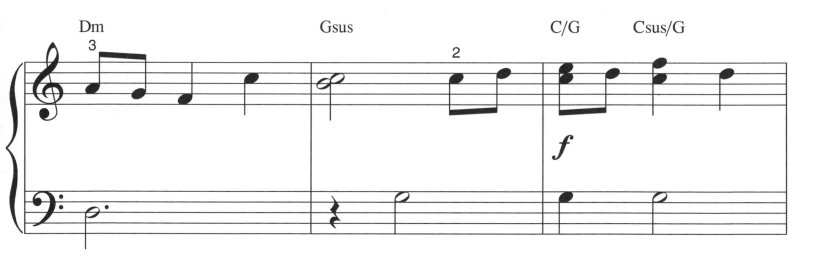

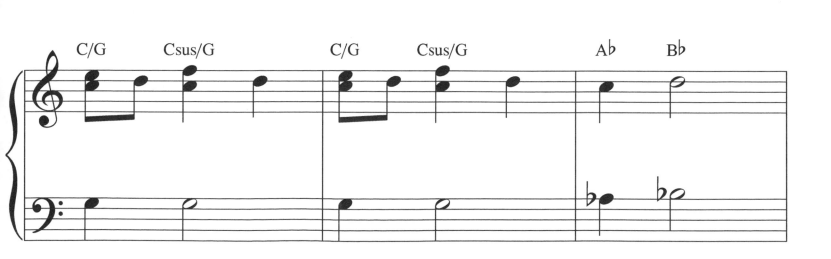

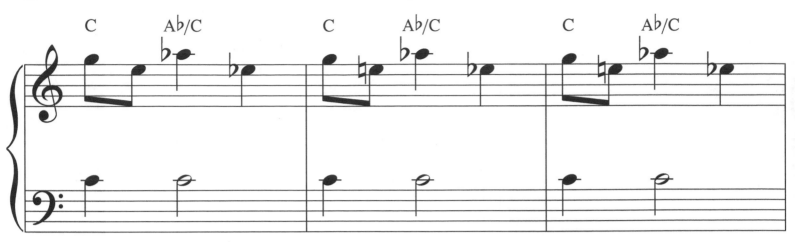

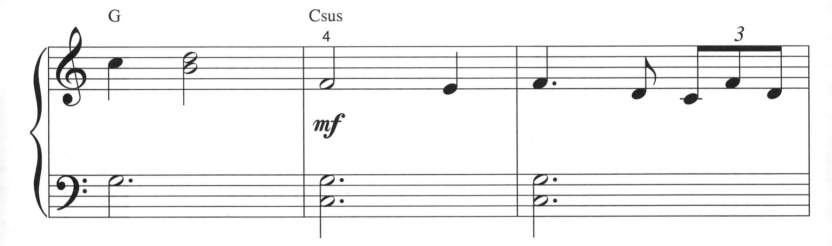

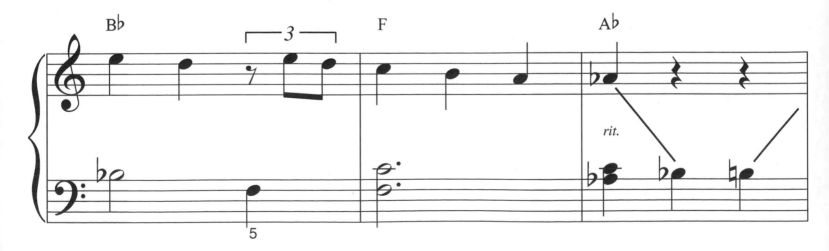

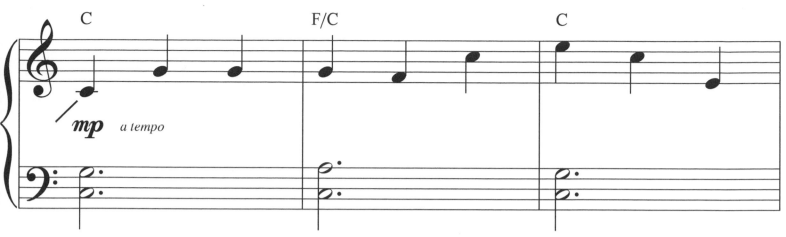

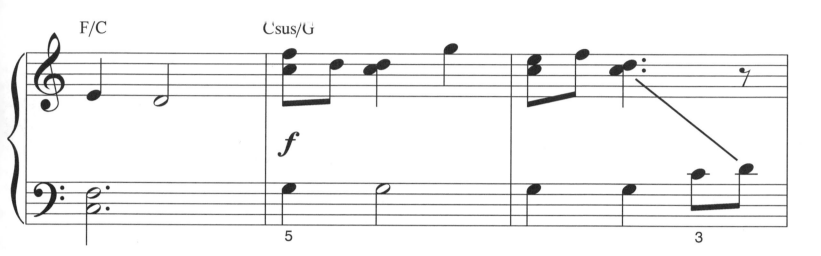

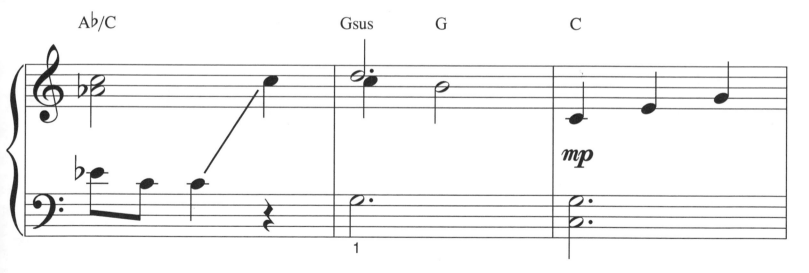

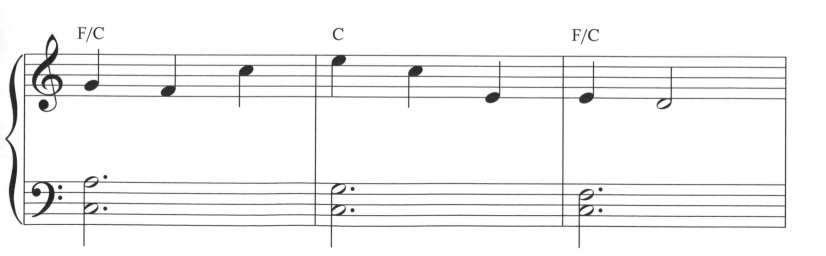

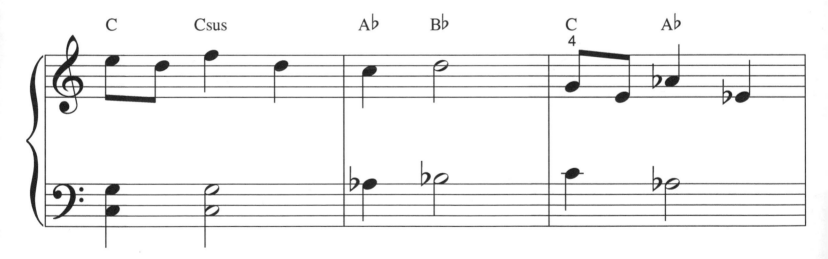

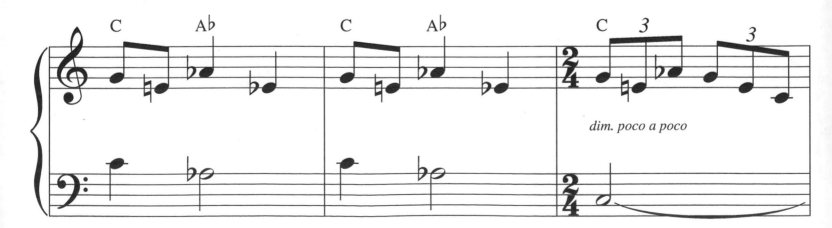

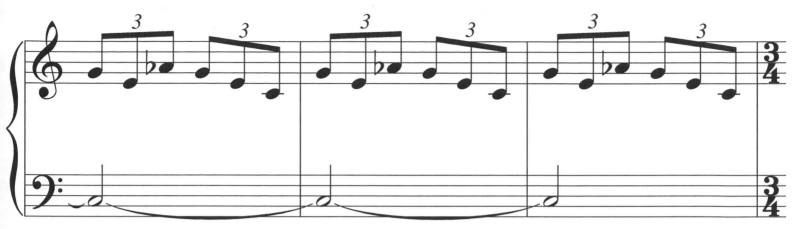

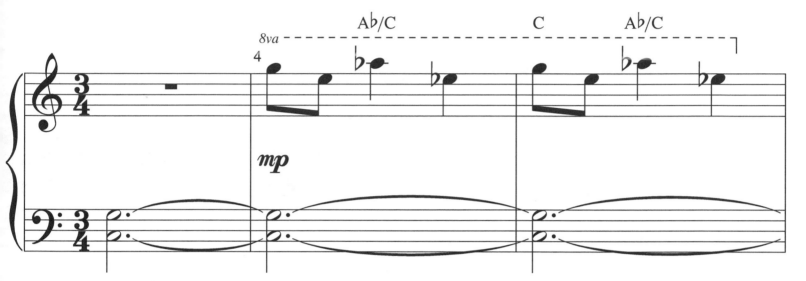

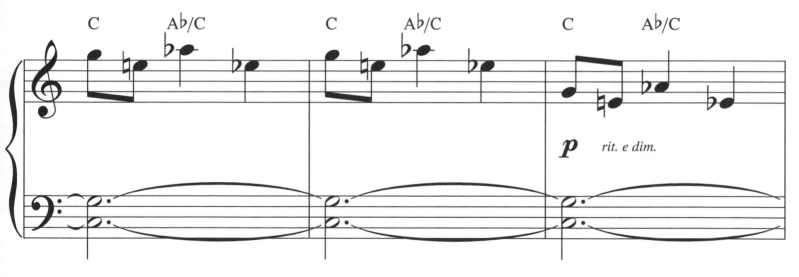

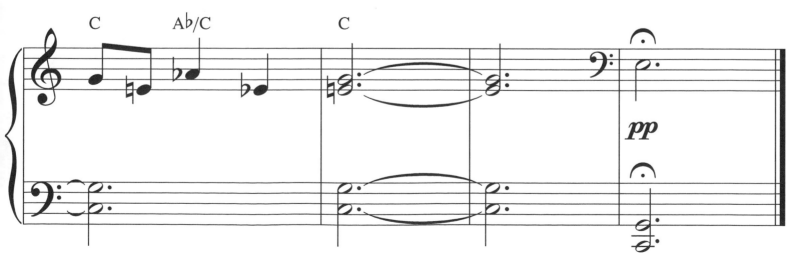

THE IMPERIAL MARCH
(Darth Vader's Theme)
from THE EMPIRE STRIKES BACK - A Twentieth Century-Fox Release

Music by JOHN WILLIAMS

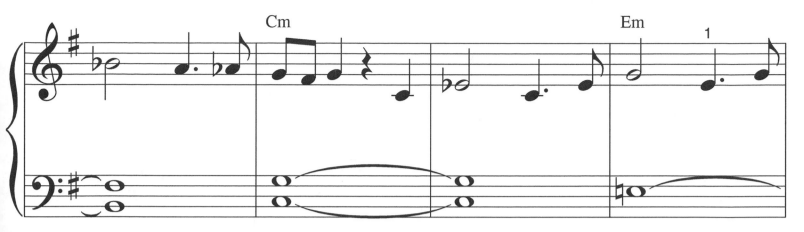

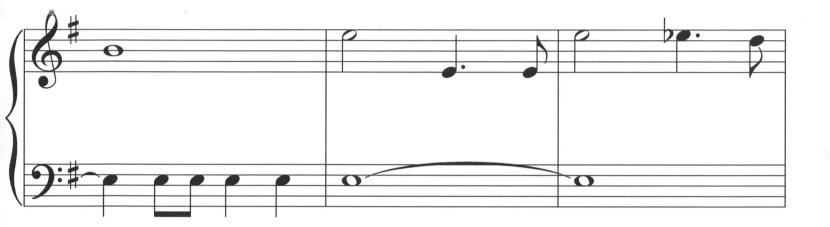

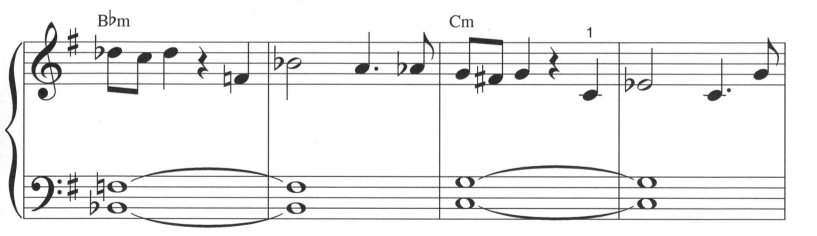

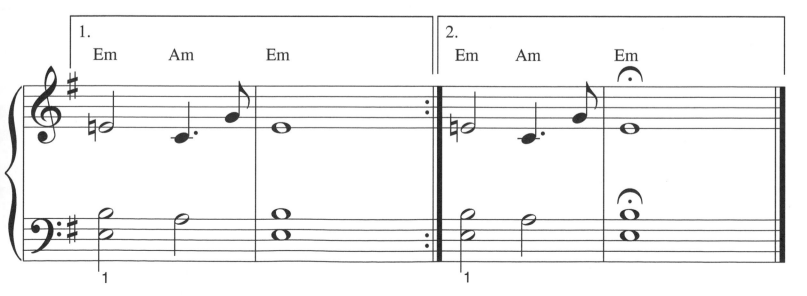

THEME FROM "JAWS"

from the Universal Picture JAWS

By JOHN WILLIAMS

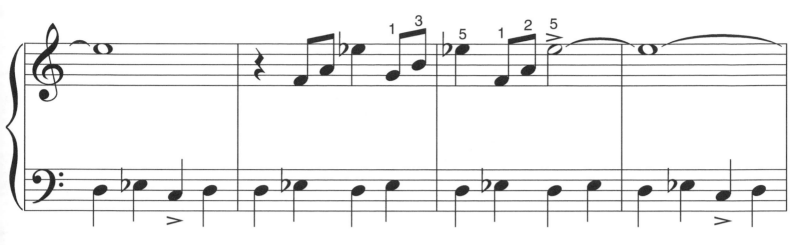

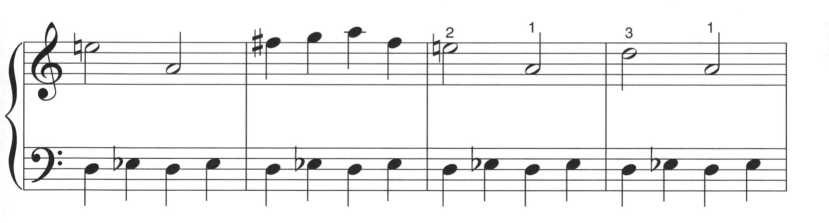

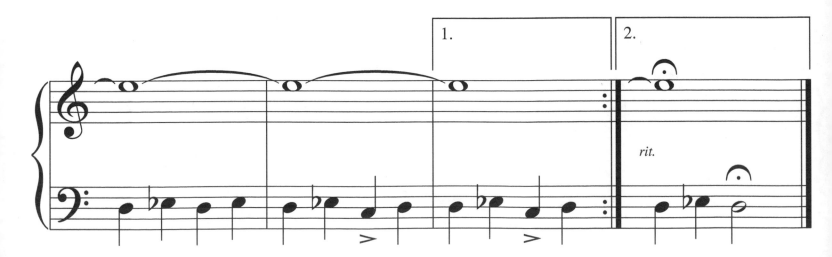

THEME FROM "JURASSIC PARK"

from the Universal Motion Picture JURASSIC PARK

Composed by
JOHN WILLIAMS

Reverently

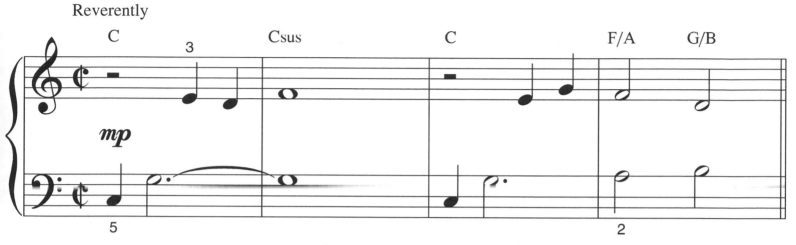

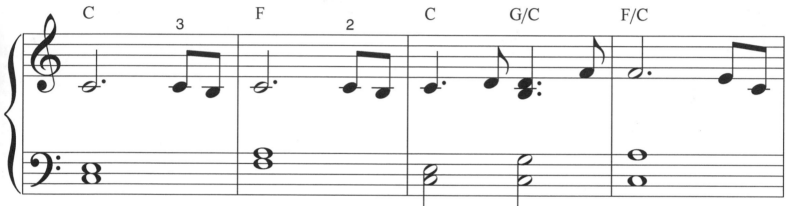

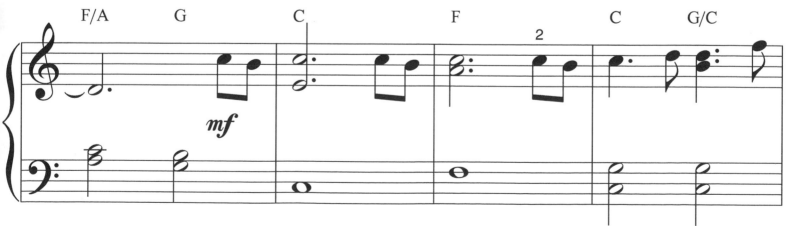

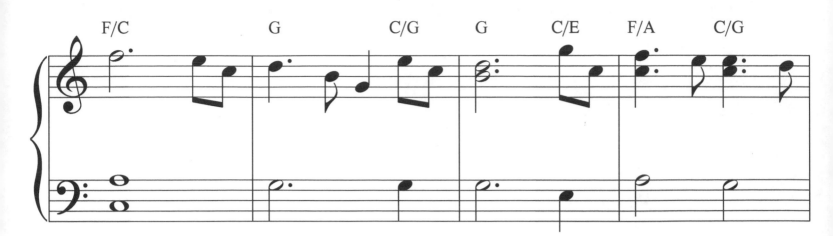

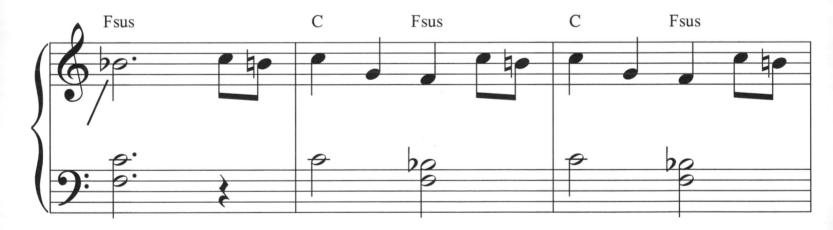

(melody)

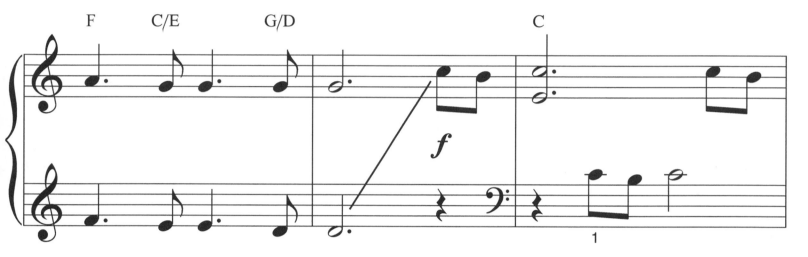
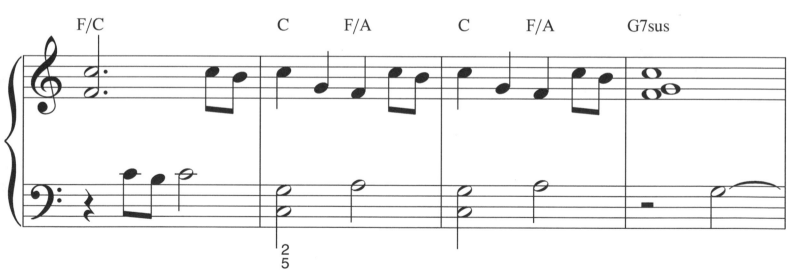
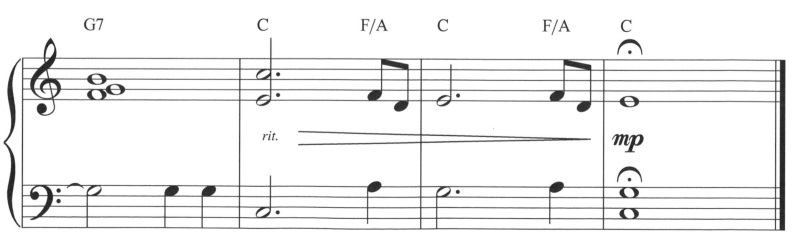

OLYMPIC FANFARE AND THEME

Commissioned by the 1984 Los Angeles Olympic Organizing Committee

Music by
JOHN WILLIAMS

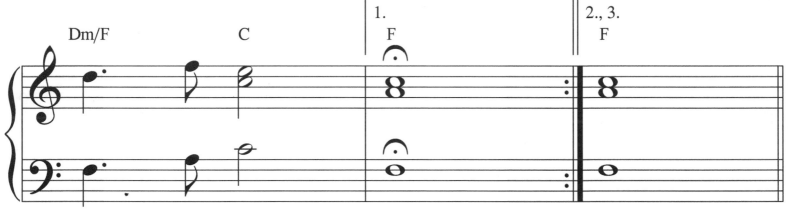

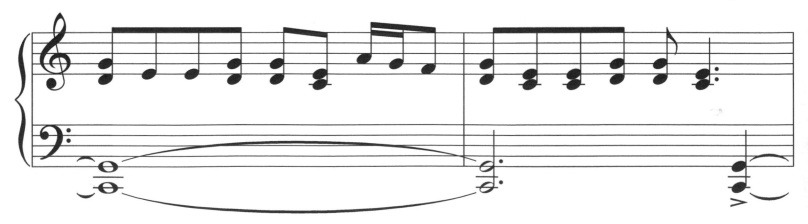

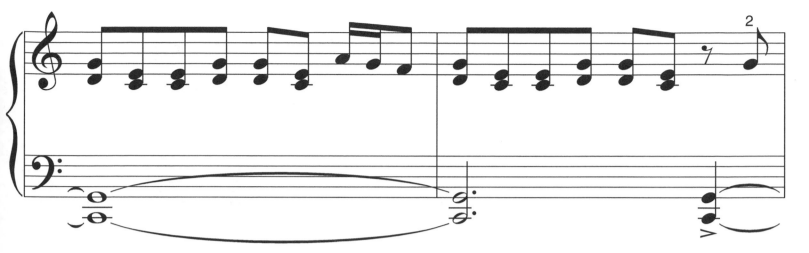

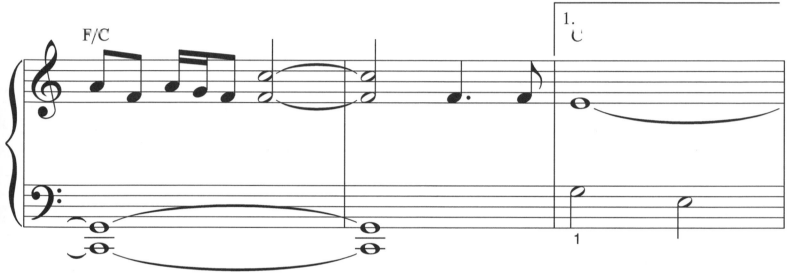

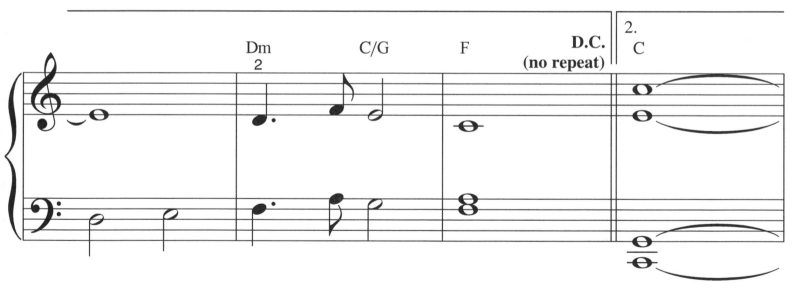

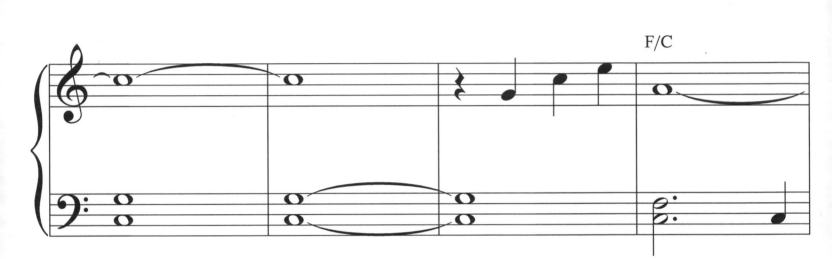

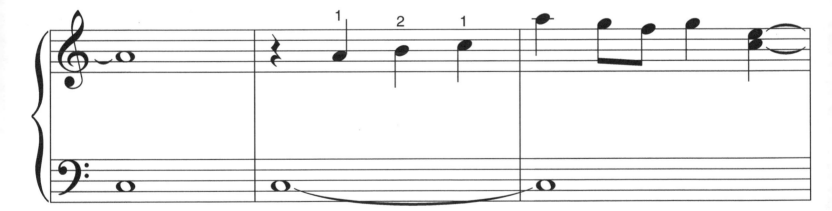

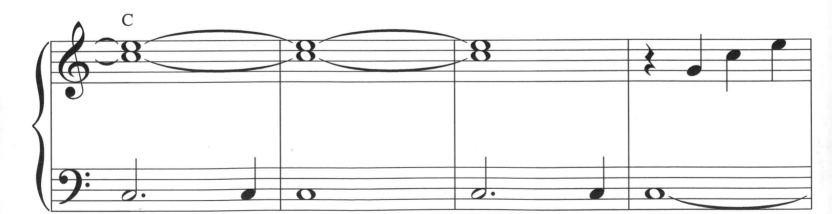

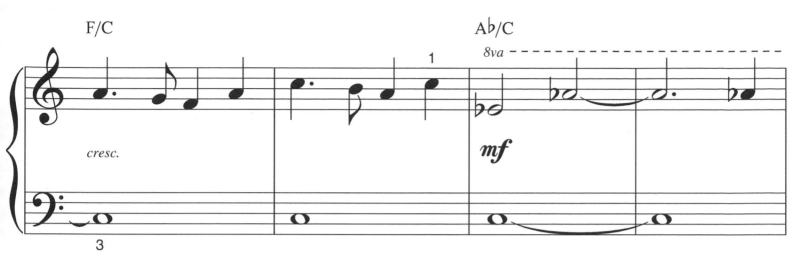

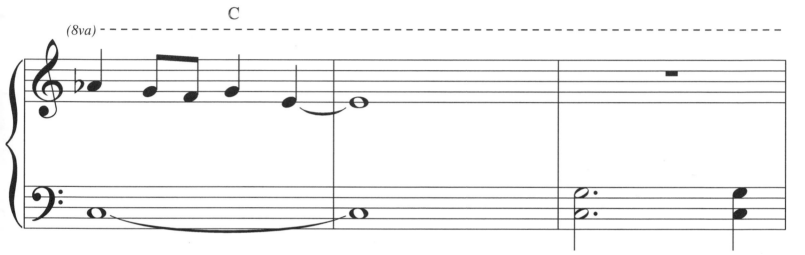

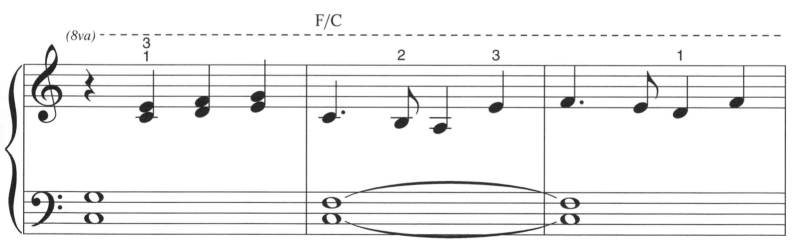

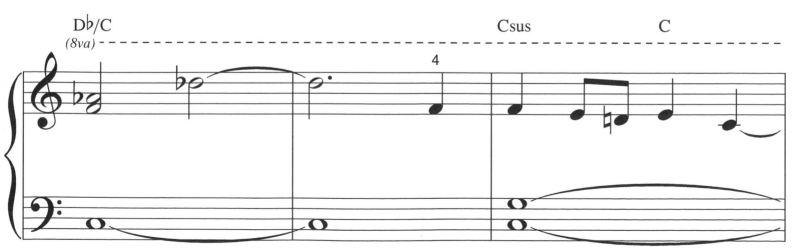

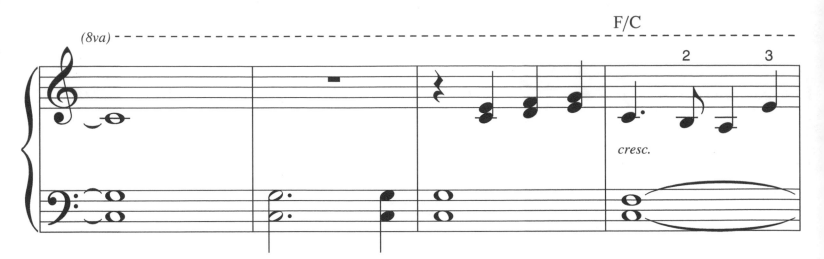

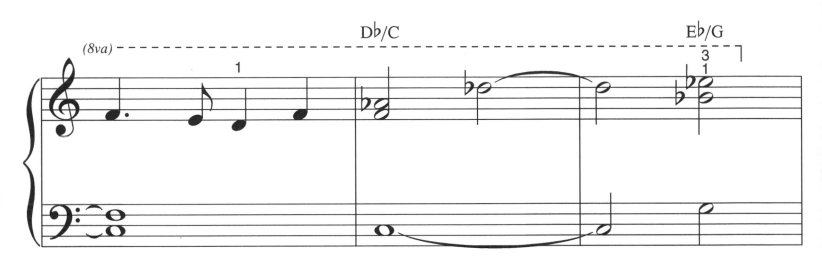

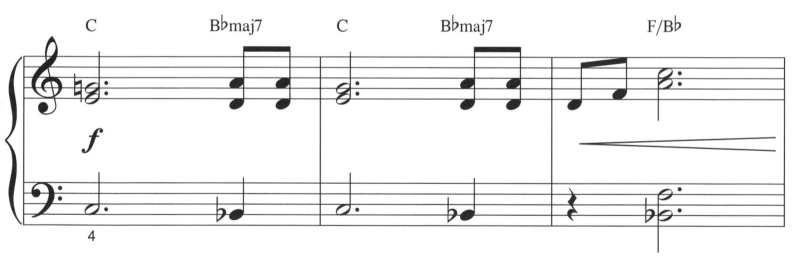

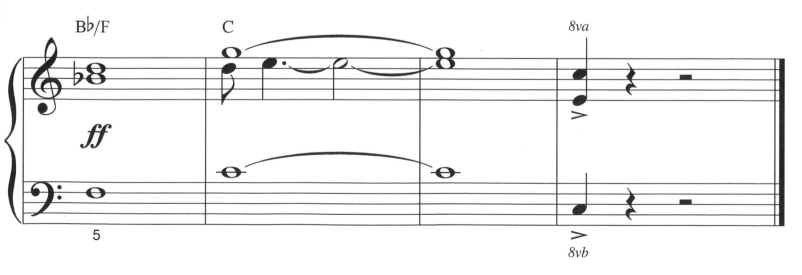

THE OLYMPIC SPIRIT
(1988 Olympic Theme)
Created for the NBC Broadcast of the 1988 Summer Olympics

Composed by
JOHN WILLIAMS

Majestically

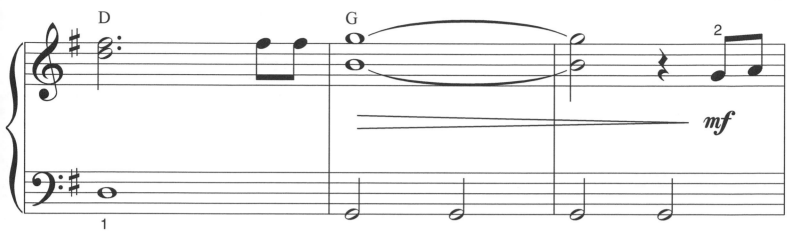

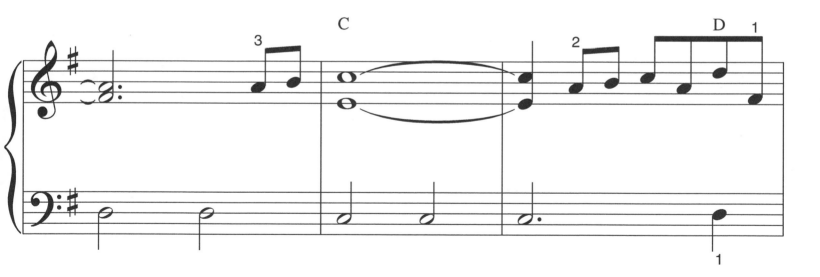

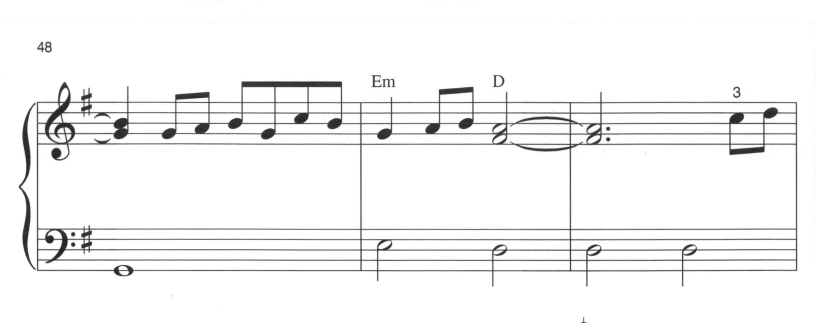

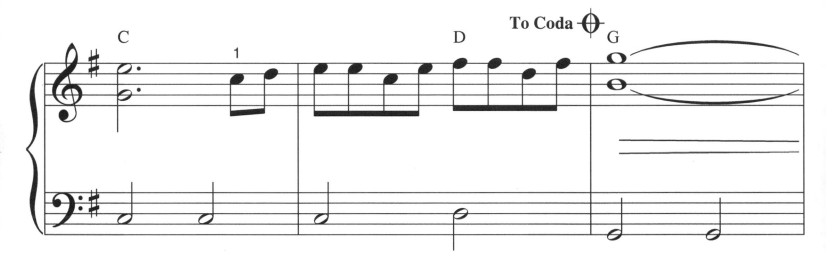

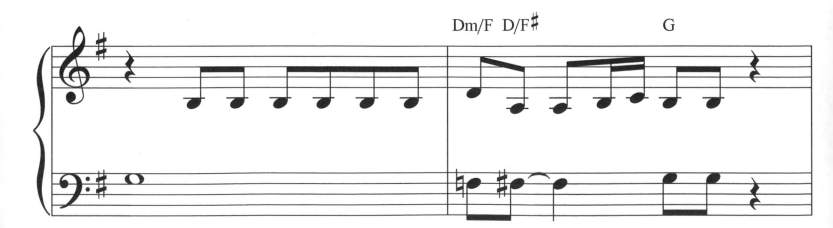

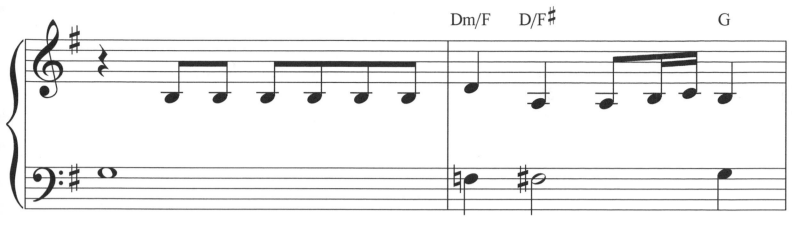

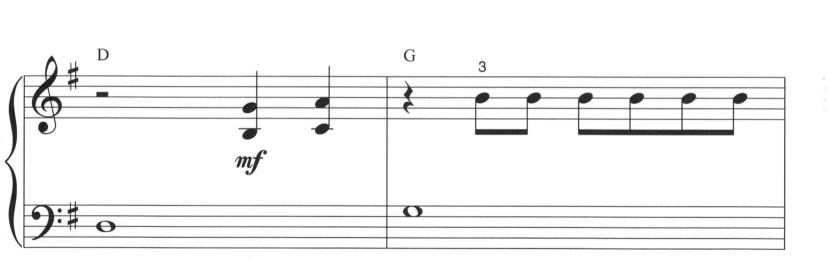

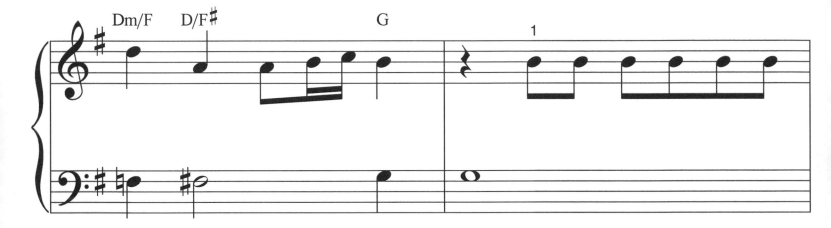

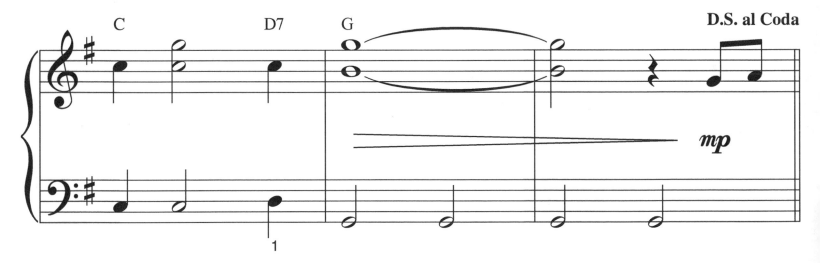

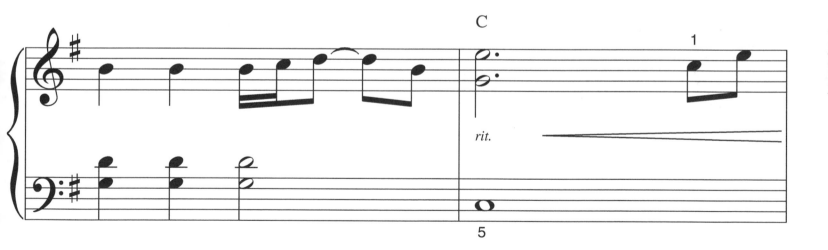

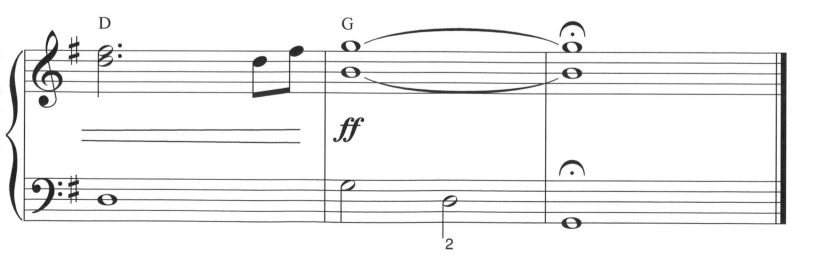

PRINCESS LEIA'S THEME

from STAR WARS® - A Twentieth Century-Fox Release

Music by
JOHN WILLIAMS

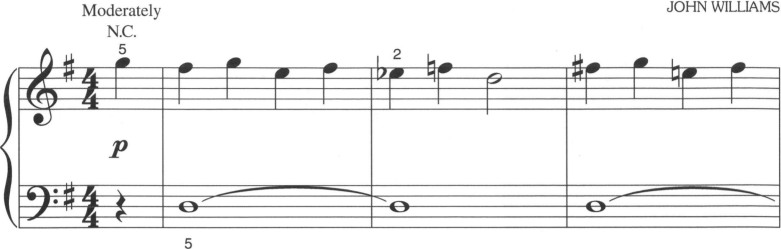

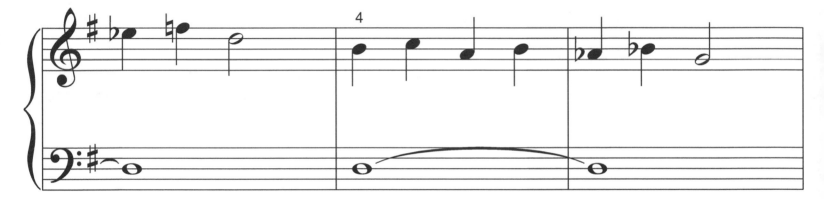

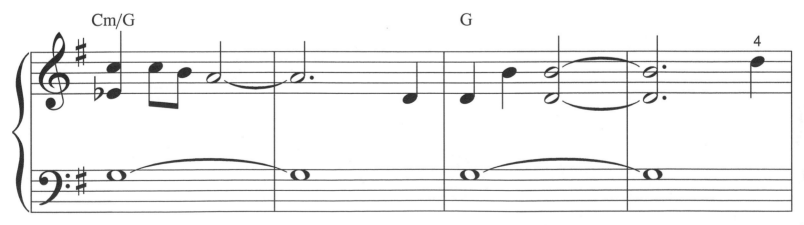

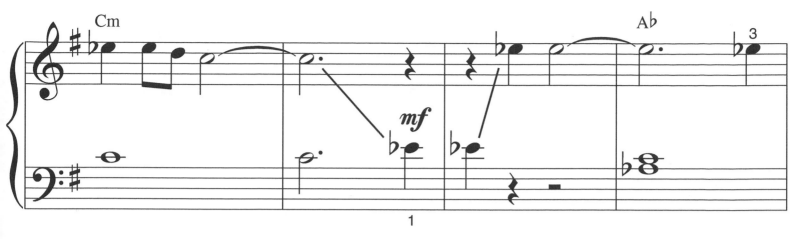

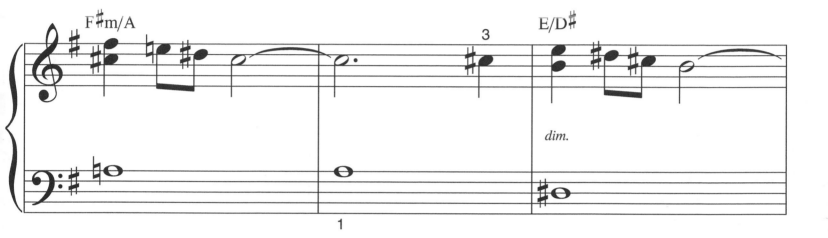

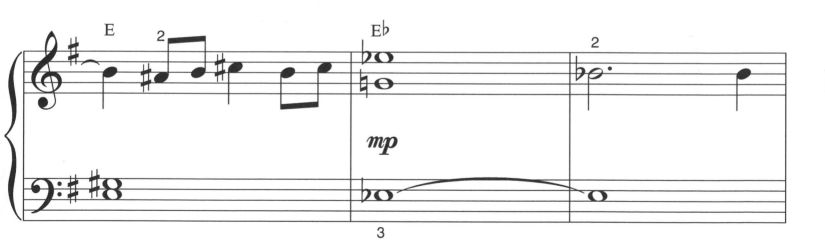

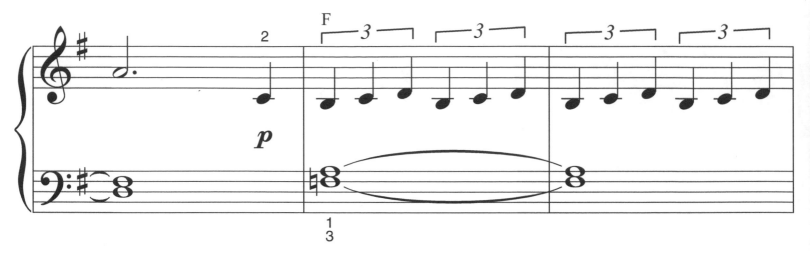

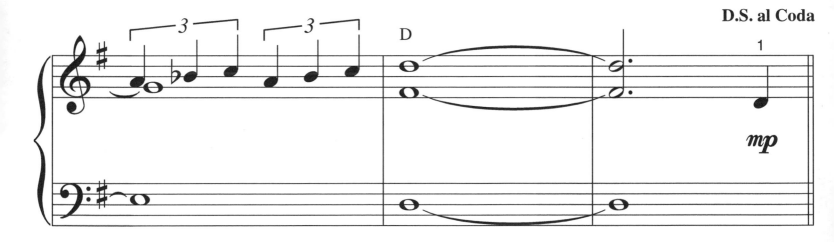

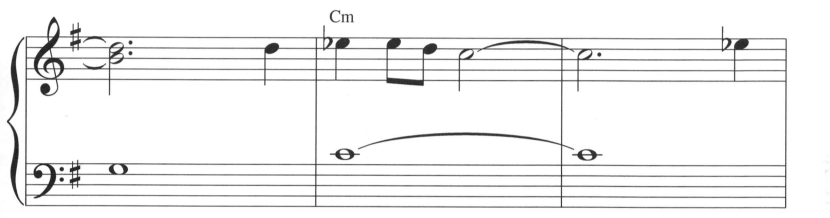

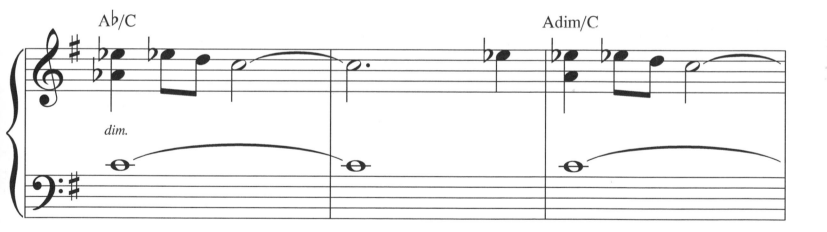

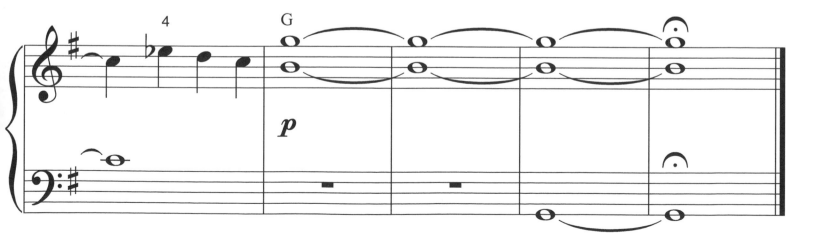

RAIDERS MARCH
from the Paramount Motion Picture RAIDERS OF THE LOST ARK

Music by
JOHN WILLIAMS

Steady March

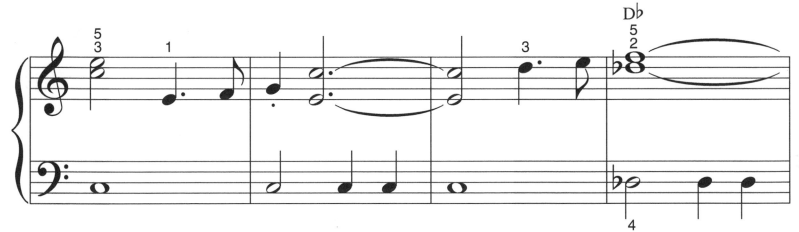

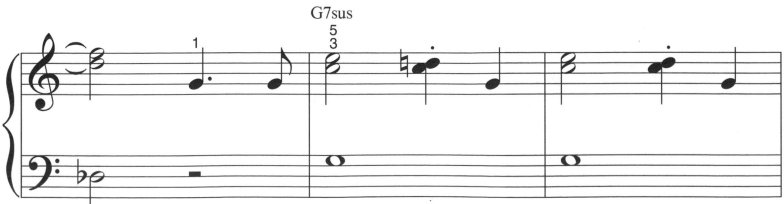

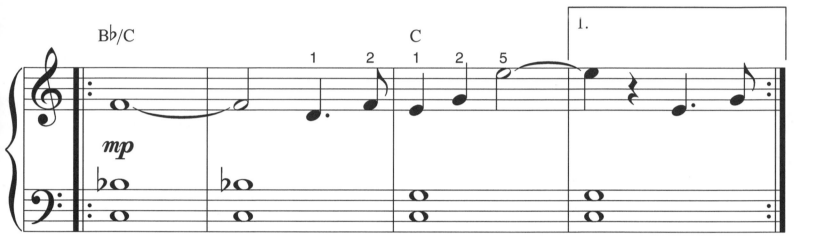

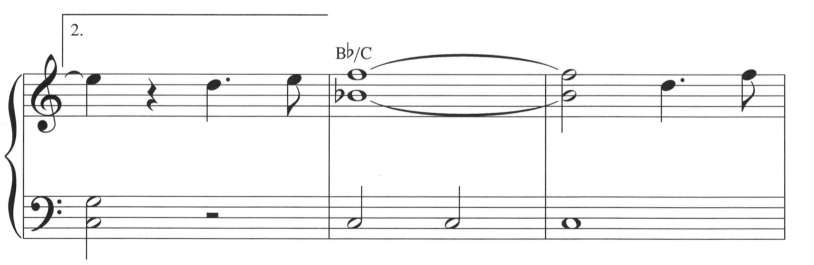

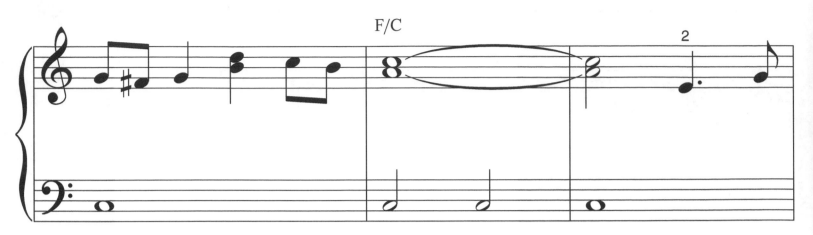

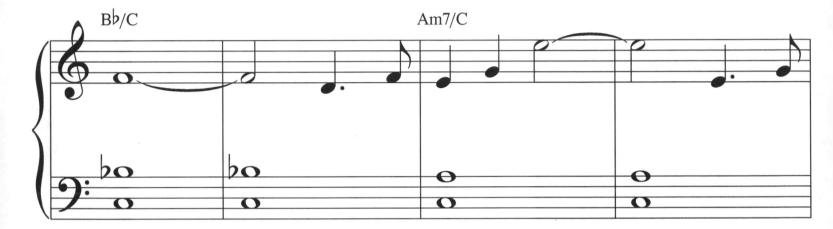

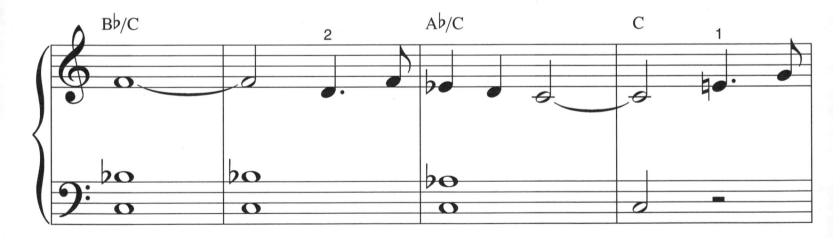

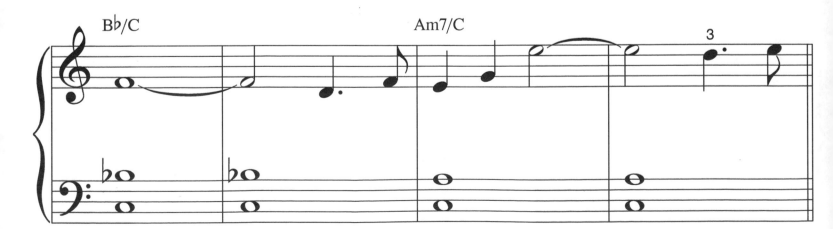

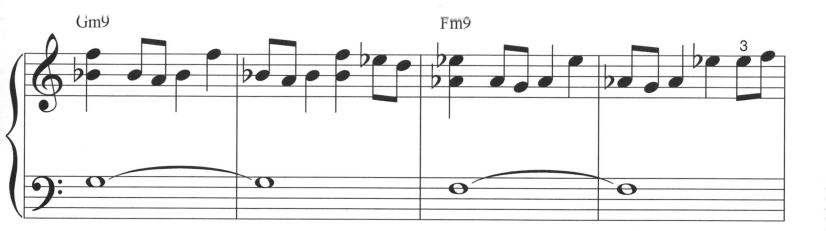

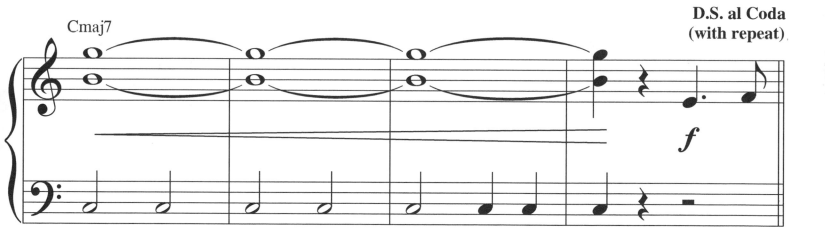

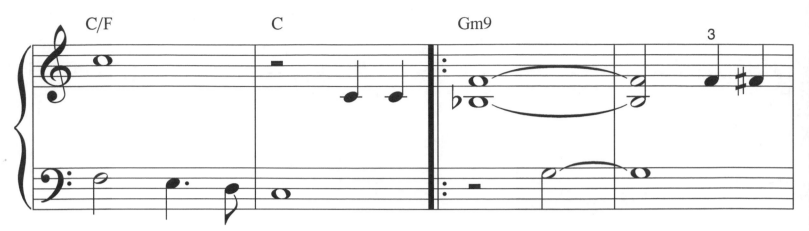

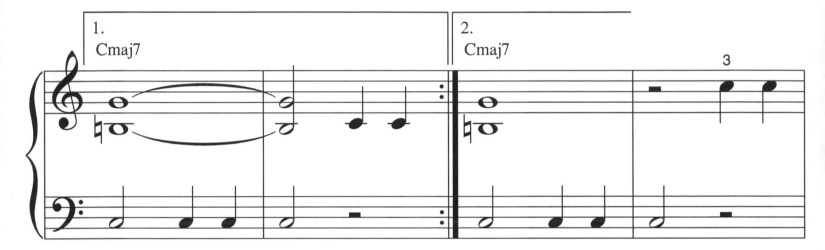

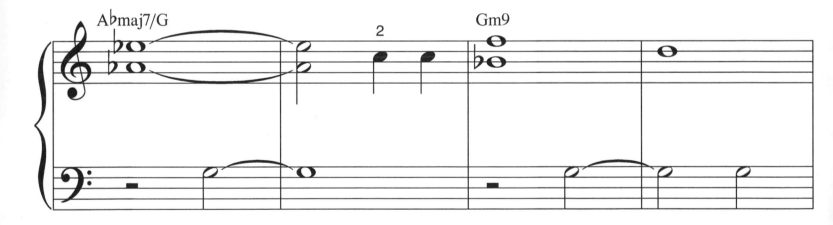

SOMEWHERE IN MY MEMORY

from the Twentieth Century Fox Motion Picture HOME ALONE

Words by LESLIE BRICUSSE
Music by JOHN WILLIAMS

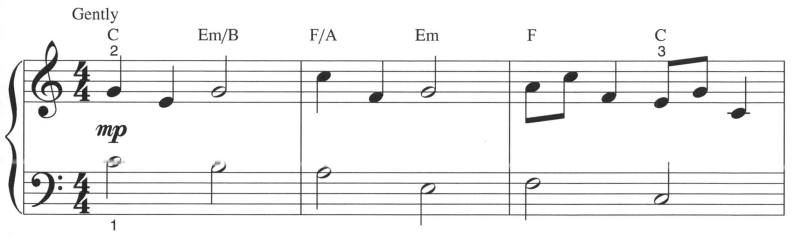

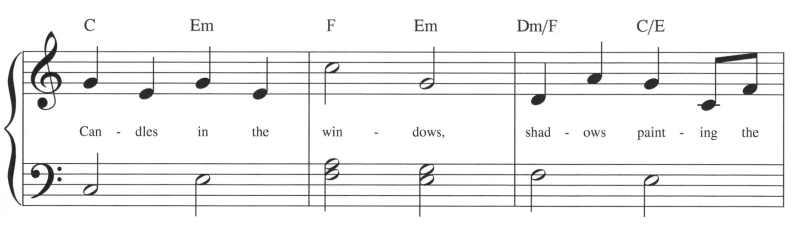

Can - dles in the win - dows, shad - ows paint - ing the

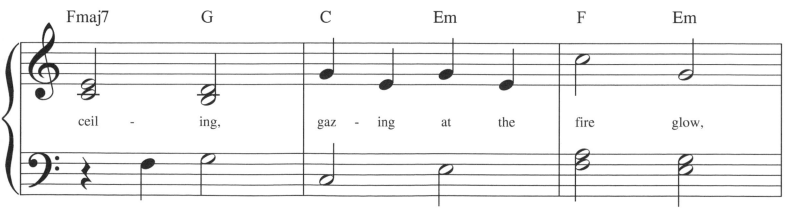

ceil - ing, gaz - ing at the fire glow,

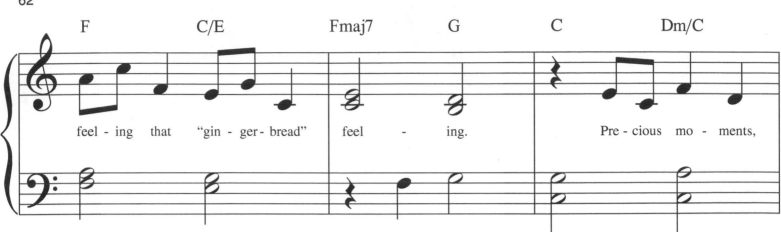

feel - ing that "gin - ger - bread" feel - ing. Pre - cious mo - ments,

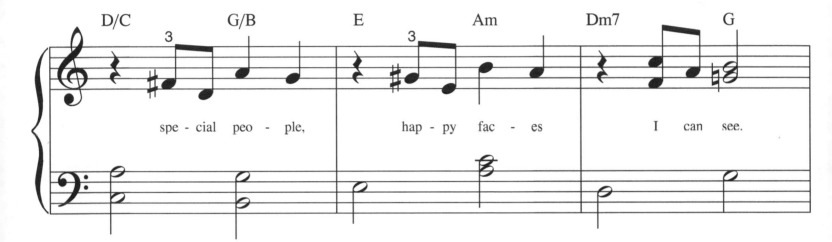

spe - cial peo - ple, hap - py fac - es I can see.

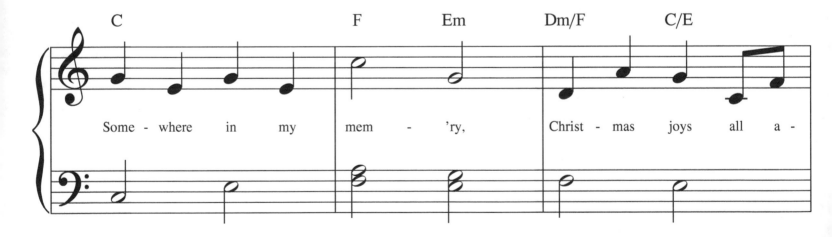

Some - where in my mem - 'ry, Christ - mas joys all a -

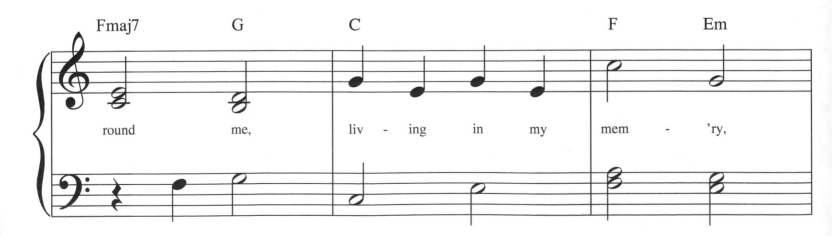

round me, liv - ing in my mem - 'ry,

all of the mu - sic, all of the mag - ic,

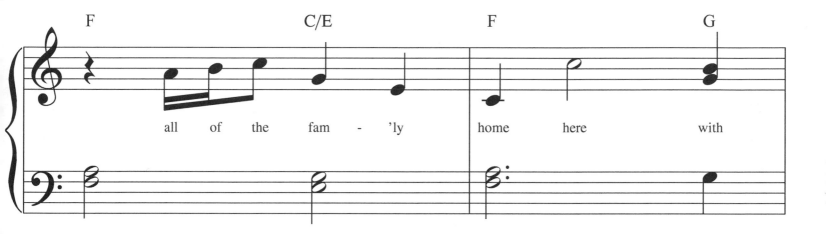

all of the fam - 'ly home here with

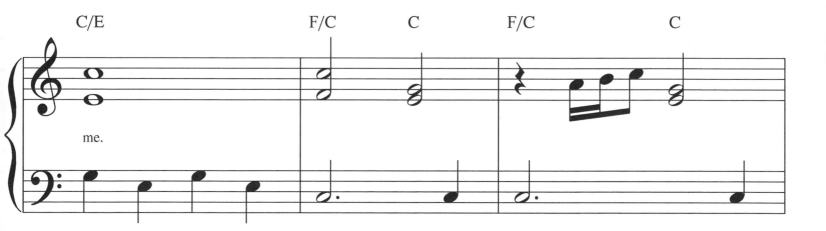

me.

rit.

THEME FROM "SCHINDLER'S LIST"

from the Universal Motion Picture SCHINDLER'S LIST

Music by
JOHN WILLIAMS

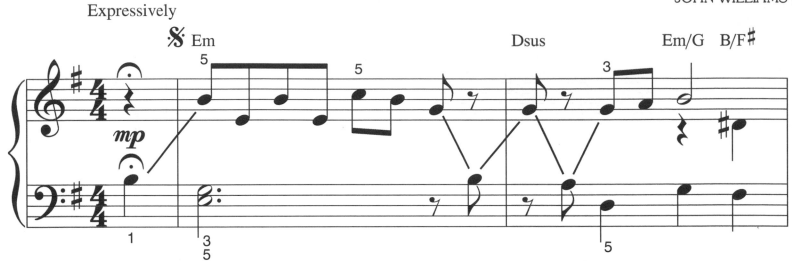

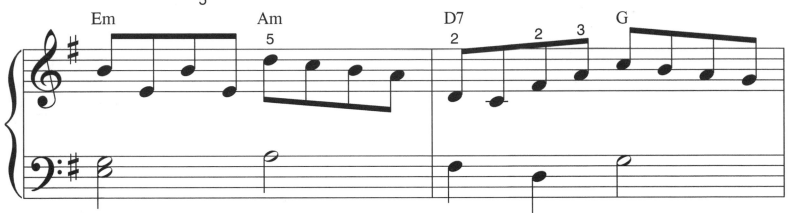

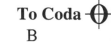

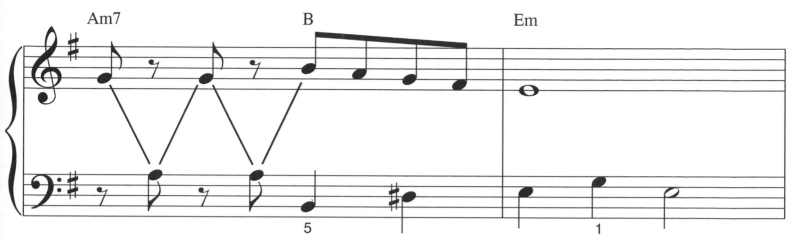

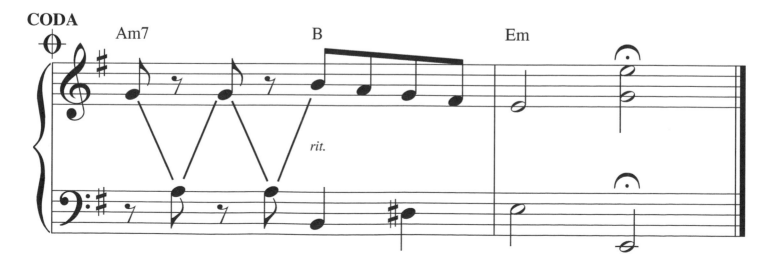

STAR WARS®
(Main Theme)
from STAR WARS, THE EMPIRE STRIKES BACK and RETURN OF THE JEDI

Music by
JOHN WILLIAMS

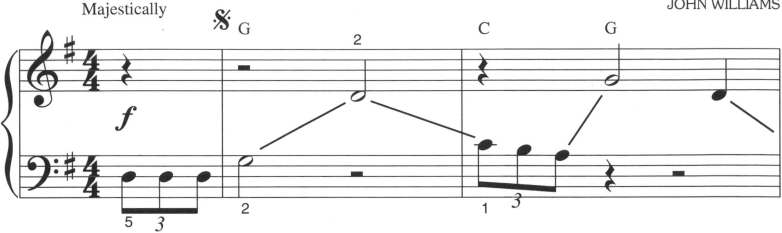

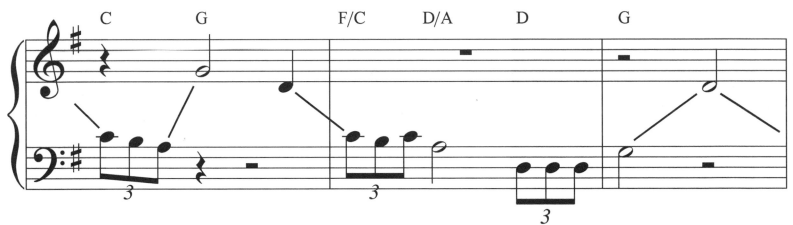

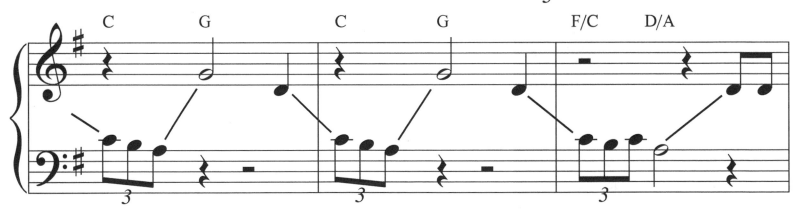

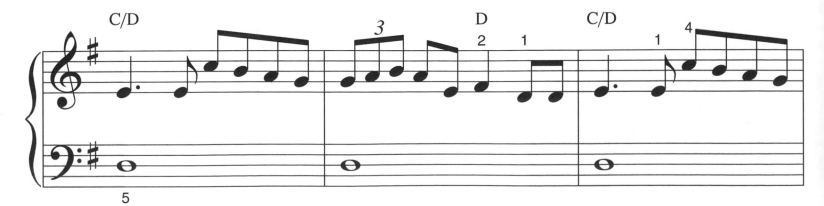

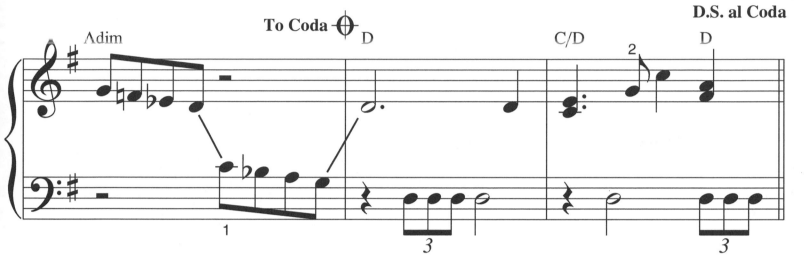

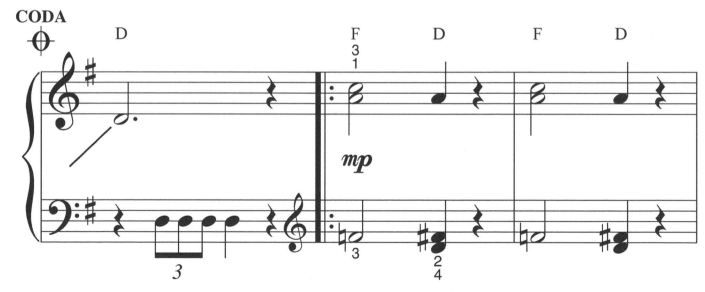

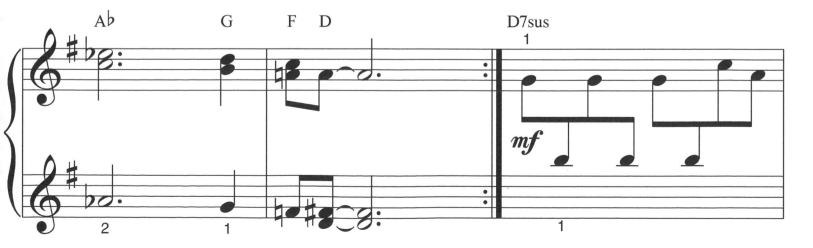

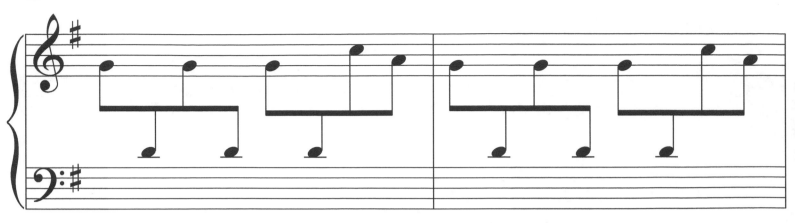

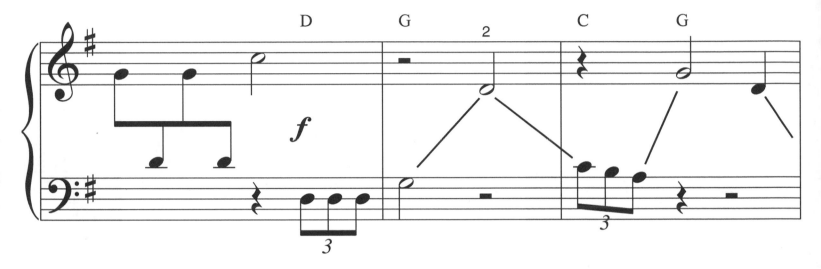

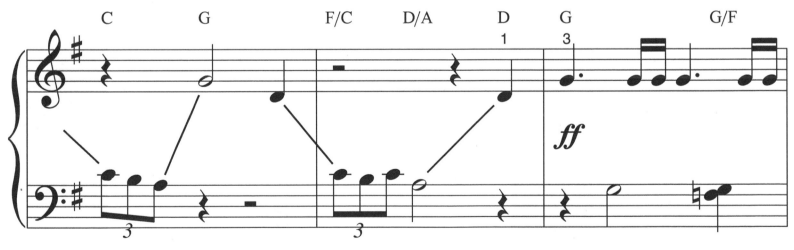

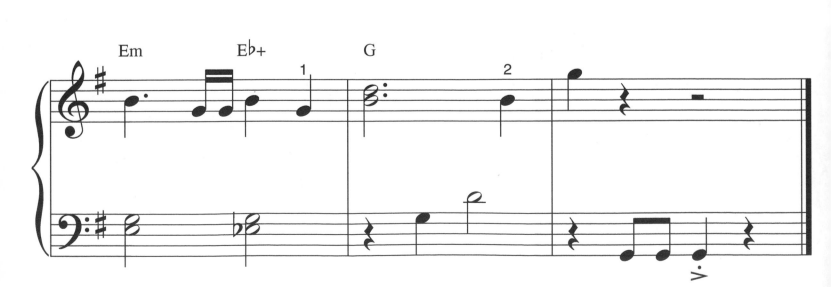

WITH MALICE TOWARD NONE

from the Motion Picture LINCOLN

Composed by
JOHN WILLIAMS

With simple expression

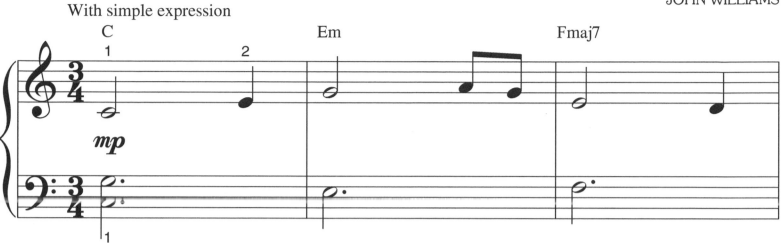

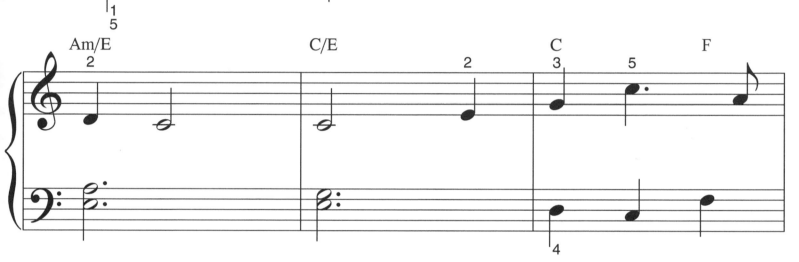

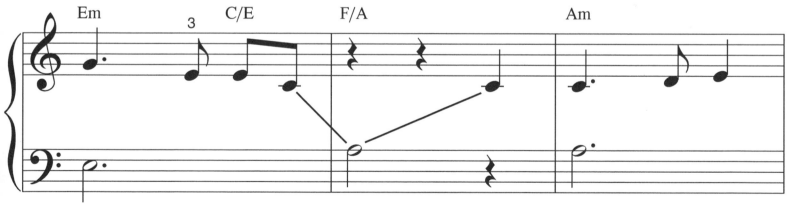

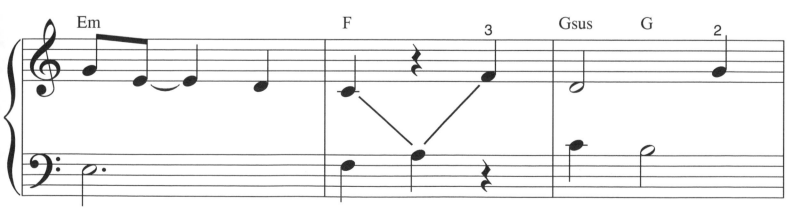

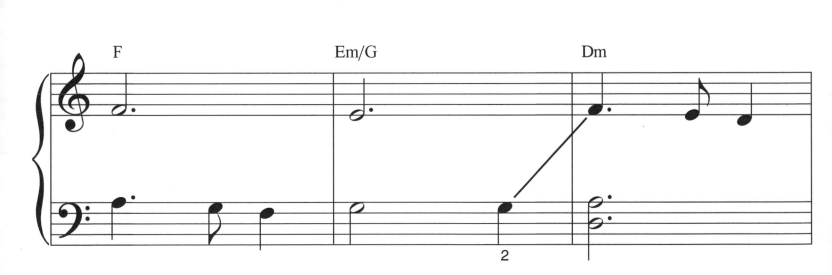

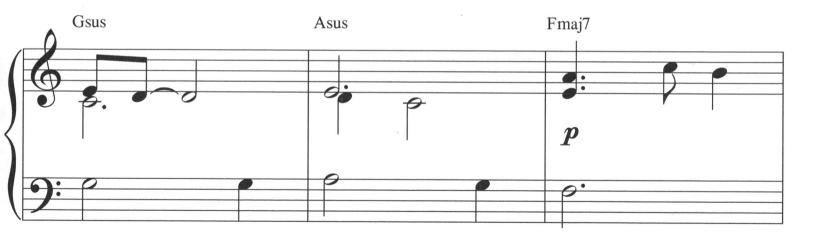

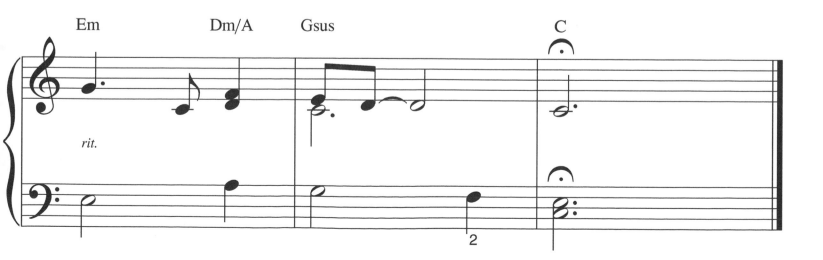